T0268429

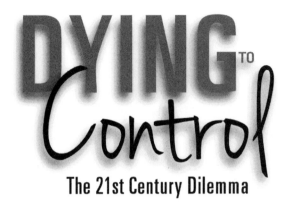

DYING TO Control

The 21st Century Dilemma

Leon R. Hayduchok

WESTBOW
PRESS
A DIVISION OF THOMAS NELSON

ISBN: 978-1-4497-5818-9 (sc)
ISBN: 978-1-4497-5819-6 (e)
ISBN: 978-1-4497-5820-2 (hc)

Library of Congress Control Number: 2012911705

WestBow Press books may be ordered through booksellers or by contacting:

WestBow Press
A Division of Thomas Nelson
1663 Liberty Drive
Bloomington, IN 47403
www.westbowpress.com
1-(866) 928-1240

Printed in the United States of America

WestBow Press rev. date: 07/31/2012

Contents

Introduction

Time was beating second after relentless second as I sat, hunkered down in my apartment study, surrounded by the workload of seminary. Mindful of a deadline that would arise shortly after dawn, I fired away at the keyboard, writing a paper on the subject of God's holiness. Having been exposed to impressions of God from an early age, I described his holiness as I had always envisioned it—a glorious light radiating his absolute power and authority throughout the universe. I defined holiness in terms of purity, perfection, and the absence of sin. Then, as I was explaining why humans cannot enter or even look upon the holy glow of God, something curious happened. Without warning, the words, "Stop writing what you already think!" blew through my mind. Silenced, I sat staring at the bright, square light of the monitor as a calming peace draped over me.

After a while I stood up, picked up my Bible, walked out of the study, sat down on the living room couch, and began reading the story that speaks to why the relationship between God and humankind is so distant—the story of Adam and Eve eating the forbidden fruit in Genesis 3.

> Now the serpent was more crafty than any of the wild animals the LORD God had made. He said to the woman, "Did God really say, 'You must not eat from any tree in the garden'?"

²The woman said to the serpent, "We may eat fruit from the trees in the garden, ³but God did say, 'You must not eat fruit from the tree that is in the middle of the garden, and you must not touch it, or you will die.'"

⁴"You will not surely die," the serpent said to the woman. ⁵"For God knows that when you eat of it your eyes will be opened, and you will be like God, knowing good and evil."

⁶When the woman saw that the fruit of the tree was good for food and pleasing to the eye, and also desirable for gaining wisdom, she took some and ate it. She also gave some to her husband, who was with her, and he ate it. ⁷Then the eyes of both of them were opened, and they realized they were naked; so they sewed fig leaves together and made coverings for themselves.

⁸Then the man and his wife heard the sound of the LORD God as he was walking in the garden in the cool of the day, and they hid from the LORD God among the trees of the garden. ⁹But the LORD God called to the man, "Where are you?"

"Where are you?" Those words caught my eye in a way they never had before, and like a child seeing fireworks for the first time, I gazed at them in fearful delight. Awed and perplexed, I began to wonder: *If sin and sinful beings cannot exist in the presence of God, then what was God doing walking in the garden of Eden* after *Adam and Eve had eaten the forbidden fruit? And why did God call out, "Where are you?"* An all-powerful, all-knowing God certainly would have been aware of what they'd done and where they were hiding. This Genesis story, credited with explaining the expanse between a holy God and a sinful humanity, actually speaks of a God who reaches out to us.

I didn't know this God, or at least I didn't understand the complexity of this God. The God of my Catholic upbringing would have yelled, "I know where you are! I know what you did! Come out and receive your just punishment!" The God of my Protestant faith would have retreated to the purity of heaven to begin bridging the chasm between a holy God and a sinful humanity. Why was I taught that sin could not exist in the presence of God? How had I missed God's invitation in verse 9 for so many years?

As I watched the foundation of my Christian faith detonate, I marveled at the glorious display. For the first time I was seeing God in color. The blinding white light of a punitive dictator who torments us for our sin had given way to a colorful array, and the silhouette of God as an alienated friend who must overcome the cosmic law that sinful beings cannot exist in his presence faded to black.

Since those dawning hours on September 23, 1998, my life has been consumed with studying, teaching, and experiencing the implications of Genesis 3. This book is a product of that journey. Written through the lens of Adam and Eve, *Dying to Control* is a reflective commentary on twentieth- and twenty-first-century American culture.

To appreciate this book, you don't have to consider the garden of Eden drama to be a historical account; all that's necessary is that you're willing to consider the possibility that the story offers some insight into humanity's conflict with God and one another. For too long now the debate between the scientific and religious communities over the historical merits of Adam and Eve and the garden of Eden has divided and distracted people from the story itself. Arguments over issues such as whether serpents ever walked or talked have grown old and have little bearing on the meaning and relevance of the account.

To illustrate my point, consider the story of the Three Little Pigs. Imagine if someone dismissed the tale because pigs do not build houses and wolves cannot blow them down. In response to the dismissal, imagine someone else trying to validate the story by providing scientific evidence suggesting that pigs may have at one time walked on two legs, had opposable thumbs, and had a brain mass capable of architectural design. Can you hear the ensuing debate over the intellectual potential of pigs and the lung capacity of wolves? None of which, by the way, would have any bearing on the moral of the story. In the end, with each side fighting to win the debate, the message of the Three Little Pigs would be lost.

To be clear, I'm not equating the story of the Three Little Pigs with the story of Adam and Eve. Rather, I'm drawing a comparison that illustrates our society's absurd treatment of the garden of Eden drama. I find it hard to believe that those who argue against the historicity of the story simply dismiss the account as a mythical tale that offers little or no insight into our human condition. I also find it hard to believe that those who argue for the historicity of the story continue to focus their attention on protecting their position against attack and dissent. The garden of Eden drama—one of the oldest and most widely cherished stories in human history—has been misused and abused in the battleground of America's culture war.

Today, across America, you'll find religious enclaves still fighting this war. Consumed by their self-preserving causes, these communities of truth fighters adhere to a theology of a God who blows down houses when we don't live by his rules. Deafened by the noise of warfare, these communities don't hear, but rather fear, the engaging words of God: "Where are you?"

⌒

Where are you?

Like Adam and Eve, we all hide among the trees when we're afraid. We congregate there with those who view the world in similar ways and welcome what they see of us. We hide and gather with like-minded people because we fear the world seeing the naked truth of who we are and what we think and the shameful deeds we've done. We fear being exposed, for once we are truly known, we realize we must face an even greater fear—the fear of rejection.

To avoid living in fear, we grope for control of our lives and surroundings. Desperate to gain control of our world and our eternal destinies, we hijack anything that might give us the power needed to exert our will. Again and again, however, in our attempts to preserve and promote self we end up killing ourselves and one another. This sad irony has been an underlying theme in human history.

So, what do we do? In a world bleeding with religious conflict, in a world coughing from pollution, in a world starving for nourishment and love, what do we do?

Lasting solutions begin with making honest evaluations of ourselves as individuals and as members of families, neighborhoods, nations, and the world community. Instead of covering our humanity, we need to interact with and seek to understand one another in the midst of our humanity. Only after we stop hiding and blaming others for the woes of our world will we be able to own and address the shame we have each brought upon the human race.

My hope for humankind in the twenty-first century is that we will emerge from the shadows of shame to experience freedom from our obsession with control. This is the kind of freedom the world needs—a freedom that releases unconditional love and compassion.

My hope for this book is that it will stimulate self-reflection and dialogue that will draw people out of hiding to experience life with one another. I also hope this book will contribute to the theological framework of the next generation of Christians who believe they have a God-given responsibility to participate in restoring an Eden-like beauty to every dark corner of our world.

In the end we have a choice—individually and collectively. We can continue fighting for control by ignoring, denying, deflecting, rationalizing, and whitewashing the truth of who we are and what we think and the shameful deeds we do—or with open and outstretched hands we can submit to one another.

Fight or submit—that is the choice set before us. That is the dilemma of dying to control.

PART I

DYING TO CONTROL

CHAPTER 1

~

DO YOU TRUST ME?

Now the serpent was more crafty than any of the
wild animals the LORD God had made. He said to
the woman, "Did God really say, 'You must not eat
from any tree in the garden'?"

²The woman said to the serpent, "We may eat
fruit from the trees in the garden, ³but God did say,
'You must not eat fruit from the tree that is in the
middle of the garden, and you must not touch it,
or you will die.'"

⁴"You will not surely die," the serpent said to the
woman. ⁵"For God knows that when you eat of it
your eyes will be opened, and you will be like God,
knowing good and evil."

—Genesis 3:1–5

FIVE OR SO years ago my wife, Anne-Marie, and I decided it was
time to take the plunge—to buy our first home. We found an
intriguing house in the foothills of the Adirondack Mountains in
central New York. The structure needed a lot of work, but it had a solid
foundation and offered a distinctive feature—a twenty-two-foot-long,

five-foot-wide, three-and-a-half-foot-deep lap pool. Buying a home with a pool would be perfect for staying in shape and getting the one little guppy we had at that time comfortable with water.

We bought the house and moved in during the summer of 2003. Since then we've survived several renovation projects, brought two more children into the world, and progressively deteriorated into the worst physical shape of our lives. I've come to understand the only kind of exercise I hate more than jogging is swimming, and Anne-Marie has developed an aversion toward any body of water with a temperature below that of a soothing, warm bath. What I'm trying to say here is that we don't use the pool as often as we'd intended.

Our two older girls, however, love to go swimming. Kirstin, who is now nearly six, can easily stand in the pool with her head above water and can just about swim from end to end without stopping. Lilia, our three-and-a-half-year-old, cannot quite reach the bottom but frolics just fine when wearing her pink floaties. Whenever I ask them if they want to go swimming, they stop whatever they're doing and jump into their bathing suits.

Even though I don't particularly like to get wet, swimming is the most enjoyable activity I do with my girls, especially when it's just the three of us. It's then that swimming morphs from an activity into an event. It begins shortly after we climb into the water. Once we're in and comfortable, I walk up to Kirstin, tap her on the shoulder, and ask, "Madam, may I please have this dance?"

Kirstin then turns to face me and answers in her most sophisticated voice, "Why of course."

That's when we hold hands, twirl about, and sing our rendition of *Dance with Me*. While we sing and dance, Lilia stands on the bottom rung of the pool ladder, glowing, waiting for her turn. They each get at least two dances, and they sometimes call for Mommy to come watch.

After dancing, the girls like to climb on and cling to their daddy. Eventually they ask if we can play games, their favorite being "dolphin," when I play the role of a dolphin while the girls take turns riding on my back as I splash from one end of the pool to the other, diving under water and surfacing over and over. Regardless of how much we've danced, how much we've played, or even how cold the girls get, the event is not complete without the girls getting at least one dolphin ride each.

I've been thinking a lot about swimming with my girls this past week, wondering why our time together in the pool is so special. My reflections have consumed me and as hard as I've tried to make them stop, my thoughts have continued to swirl. During these obsessive episodes, my mind slips into slow-motion replay, recounting the events of the previous Saturday when I faltered as a father.

It happened when Kirstin, Lilia, and I were in the pool, just the three of us. Mommy and five-month-old Annika were taking a nap. Lilia had just finished a dolphin ride and had stepped onto the ladder as Kirstin boarded my back. Once Kirstin was in place, dolphin took off, leaving Lilia alone on the ladder, anxiously waiting for her next turn.

When Kirstin and I arrived at the other end of the pool and turned around, Kirstin called out "Lilia!" I looked up, but without my glasses I couldn't see very well. I could make out only a little something in the water next to the ladder. As I rushed the length of the pool I could see it was Lilia—motionless—with just the top of her head at the surface.

I raised my Sunshine up out of the water. Lilia's eyes were closed, water spilled from her mouth, and she was out. As I sat her on the concrete deck, I repeatedly smacked her back, crying out her name again and again, "Lilia! Lilia! Lilia!"

In those seconds between Kirstin calling out her sister's name and my sitting Lilia on the deck, thoughts and questions rushed through my mind: *What? Where's Lilia? That can't be her! Oh God, that is her! She must be okay! She's not moving! This can't be happening! How long could it have been? It couldn't have been that long! She can't be dead!*

After a few smacks on the back Lilia began to cough and throw up water. Once she could breathe, Lilia stood up and began to scream; I think she was returning to the fear she'd felt just before she'd blacked out. Hoping to comfort her, I stretched out my arms, and without hesitation my little Lilia jumped to me. As I squeezed her close to my chest I could feel my love wash over her. I was so scared—scared by how much I loved her, scared by how much it would have hurt to have lost her.

Once we calmed down, I asked her if she was okay. She nodded. Then I asked, "What happened?"

Lilia attempted to speak but could respond with only a sobbing cry. Eventually she muttered, "I tried to call out 'Daddy,' but I couldn't."

Speechless, I just hugged my Sunshine as we wept together.

Later, when Anne-Marie woke up, I told her what had happened. Her eyes welled up as I recounted the story. When I told her about Lilia jumping back into my arms, Anne-Marie was surprised that Lilia would so quickly return to the water. She asked me why I thought Lilia was not afraid to get back in.

As I thought about that question, my emotions surfaced again.

In that moment I realized there was no other human being on the planet who trusts me the way Lilia trusts me. Annika, who cannot swim, has no choice in whether or not to trust. Kirstin, exploring the waters of self-sufficiency, is learning about distrust. And Anne-Marie, a strong swimmer, understands the complexities of trust. Lilia, with the faith of a child, freely chose to jump back into her daddy's arms, believing he was perfect and knew everything.

Overwhelmed by Lilia's trust in me, my mind began to churn in unforgiving surf.

After a week of obsessive contemplation, I better understood why swimming with my girls is so special; it offers us the opportunity to affirm our bond of trust. Although Kirstin and Lilia are becoming more at ease in the pool, they still look to their daddy to protect them from the threats of the water. Their proclamations, "Daddy, hold me, hold me!" express their desire for Daddy's care. They cling to Daddy's chest and back to feel protected; I hold them close to revel in my role as their protector. We experience the bond of our daddy-daughter relationship more intensely in our pool than we ever do in the safety of our living room or on the lawn outside. That's why it's so much fun. That's why it's so special.

As the girls get older, my trust relationship with each of them will evolve and become increasingly complex. Turbulent seas will at times weaken and maybe even threaten our bonds of trust. Yet despite the uncertainty, I hope that whatever course each daddy-daughter adventure takes we'll hold onto an undying commitment to one other.

As long as the parent-child relationship exists, as long as the ride lasts with my girls, there will be this essential, ever-present, unspoken question: "Do you trust me?"

I hope to be trustworthy.

I hope my daughters answer, "Yes."

"Do you trust me?" is the central question of personal relationships. Trust is what binds people together. The extent to which we experience trust with one another will determine the depth of each relationship. For example, we typically proclaim our love to another only after we've gained a level of confidence that the other will gently handle such sensitive news. Once we express our love, we wait in exposed anticipation to see how it's received. If it's handled well, we deem the water safe for experiencing deeper expressions of trust.

Yet regardless of how safe we feel in any personal relationship, exhibiting trust assumes certain risks. Whether we trust someone with privileged information, material goods, or our lives, to trust is to run the risk of being betrayed, rejected, or maybe even abandoned. Personal relationships do not come with any contractual guarantees. Once formal agreements enter a relationship, that aspect of the relationship is defined by impersonal terms. There is no way to escape the fact that investing in personal relationships demands personal risk.

Given the uncertainty of personal relationships, it's reasonable to question whether they are worth pursuing. What if a person, after being betrayed or abandoned, concludes that engaging in personal relationships is just not worth the risk?

Simon and Garfunkel's song *I Am a Rock* speaks to the decision to steer clear of personal relationships:

> I've built walls,
> A fortress deep and mighty,
> That none may penetrate.
> I have no need of friendship; friendship causes pain.
> It's laughter and it's loving I disdain.
> I am a rock,
> I am an island.

As the lyrics suggest, by avoiding personal relationships we can reduce personal risk and relational uncertainty. Yet is it worth it? Living in a fortress may offer us more safety and control, but is life behind walls a fulfilling human experience? Rocks may feel little relational pain as they are steady and stable and express no emotion, but is a rocklike existence enjoyable? Islands may feel little disappointment, as they are self-sufficient, never asking for or needing help from anyone, but is becoming an island unto oneself rewarding?

As much as we might not want to believe or admit it, we need one another. Humans don't do well in isolation for extended periods of time. Alone too long on a desolate island, we'll create imaginary friends and give life to inanimate objects to avoid the perils of loneliness. Add confinement to solitude, and it's only a matter of time before a person drifts into insanity.

We humans need personal interaction because we are relational beings. Connecting with others physically, intellectually, emotionally, and even spiritually is essential for our health and survival. However, we should not view human connections as simply a means to an end. If we view relationships only as interactions that help each of us to fulfill our individual goals and maximize our individual potential, then we've reduced personal relationships to impersonal exchanges of goods and services. Having such a utilitarian, narcissistic worldview undermines the essence of being human, transforming us from *human beings* into *human doings*.

Tragically, this reduction has become a central tenet of American ideology.

> The "I" is at the heart of Western religion and psychology. ... Americans grow up believing the individual is at the center of the universe. ...
>
> The single most important pattern in the United States is *individualism*. Broadly speaking, individualism refers to the doctrine, spelled out in detail by the seventeenth-century English philosopher John Locke, that each individual is unique, special, completely different from all other individuals, and "the basic unit of nature." The basic premise of Locke's view is a simple one: the interests

of the individual are or ought to be paramount, and that all values, rights, and duties originate in individuals. This emphasis on the individual, while found elsewhere in the world has emerged as the cornerstone of American culture. [1]

In viewing relationships from a vantage point of self-interest, we numb our human sensibilities of commitment and responsibility to one another. Rabid individualism further leads us to interpret life, liberty, and the pursuit of happiness as entitlements, regardless of how our pursuits might impact those around us and the world at large. Conscious of our self-centered pursuits as human doings, we interact with a spirit of skepticism and distrust. To protect our own interests, we exchange personal relationships for the control offered by impersonal relationships; it's easier to trust in the perceived certainty of a contract or a law than to trust in the integrity and loyalty of a fellow human doing.

Impersonal relationships now dominate our society. Buying a product without a contract or written guarantee is seen as foolish or naïve. Privacy fences in our suburban communities allow us to ignore our neighbors. A conversation without purposeful intent is considered lost time. Productivity, productivity, productivity is our consuming obsession. Who has the time, energy, or interest to just *be* with other people? What a waste—right?

The exchange of personal for impersonal relationships has not just affected our human interactions. The exchange has transcended into the God-human realm as well. In American society, we generally view our relationship with God as a contractual exchange of products and services. We try to live by the rules of our respective faiths while God doles out rewards and punishments in response to our successes and failures in meeting the terms of the agreement.

For those who claim to have a personal relationship with God, tragedy can quickly reveal how impersonal that relationship may actually be. The common expressions "What did I do to deserve this?" and "God, what do you want from me?" question whether I (or maybe God) failed to meet some requirement of the God-human contract. Prayer during times of trial can also sound impersonal. Take for example these timeless, fill-in-the-blank prayers of desperation: "God, if you _____, I'll never _____ again"; "God, if you _____, I promise to _____"; and "God, what do you want me to do for you to _____?" Such prayers do not sound like personal appeals to God; instead, they sound like attempts to negotiate a new contract with an old business partner.

Even the Christian message of salvation is often couched as an impersonal business transaction: sin is defined as human breaches of the original God-human contract, Jesus' death on the cross is explained as God's gracious offer to remunerate for our transgressions, and salvation is proclaimed as God's new deal. Just trust in Jesus—accept his payment on your behalf—and you're back in business with God, you're born again!

This businesslike, born-again brand of Christianity now dominates the religious landscape of twenty-first-century America. The marketing of this God-product, however, has changed significantly from its original eighteenth-century version. Back then, evangelists traveled from town to town, proclaiming that every individual must personally respond to God's new deal or upon death endure the punishment of eternal hell. With the rationale that the ends justified the means, evangelists used hard-sell tactics of intimidation and pressured people for an immediate decision to buy now or pay later. This movement began an American revolution of recontextualizing Christianity as a strictly individualistic faith.

Today's born-again product is packaged to appeal more to the felt needs of the American consumer. Initially conceived by baby boomers for baby boomers, this redesign of the born-again brand has grown into a national phenomenon and is now available across the country in various models and colors. Marketing for God's new deal seeks to draw people into bright and comfortable showrooms. Every potential buyer is welcomed at the door with a handshake and a smile, while specially trained greeters offer to take new customers on a tour of the facilities, hoping to impress them with the multitude of spiritual goods and services. Worship bands play contemporary Christian music to create an uplifting atmosphere, and testimonials proclaiming the benefits of God are showcased to develop the need and to try to build "trust," with the occasional celebrity testimony adding credibility the line of God-products. Then, when the time comes to make the sale, the senior manager preaches a user-friendly message and closes with an irresistible deal: at no cost to you he guarantees eternal, personal (that is, individualistic), heavenly bliss in return for simply trusting in Jesus.

With "I" at the heart of Western religion and psychology and with the belief that the individual is at the center of the universe, we are gradually losing our identity as relational beings. Achieving financial freedom and self-sufficiency in every imaginable aspect of life has become the American dream, with even God being portrayed as a means for reaching our own individualistic ends.

In our ongoing quest to realize the supremacy of "I," we drift away from one another. Forgoing the trust needed to experience personal relationships, we each set our sights on reaching an island of self-idolatry. The journey may get lonely at times, but visions of paradise inspire us to stay afloat.

I sometimes wonder what life would be like if I ever reached my island. Stranded and alone, how long would it take for me to start creating imaginary friends?

So what is the nature of the God-human relationship? Is it personal or impersonal? Is the relationship defined by terms in a contract or is there a personal commitment between God and humankind established through a bond of trust?

The first three chapters of Genesis speak about the birth of the cosmos, life on earth, and the fundamental relationship between God and humankind. These chapters portray God as the sovereign Creator of the physical world and as the sole Giver of life. In these creation accounts we find the use of general terms such as heaven, earth, land, water, plants, animals, and so forth. It is not until verse 8 of chapter 2 that the story moves from the general to the specific.

> [8]Now the LORD God had planted a garden in the east, in Eden; and there he put the man he had formed. [9]And the LORD God made all kinds of trees grow out of the ground—trees that were pleasing to the eye and good for food. In the middle of the garden were the tree of life and the tree of the knowledge of good and evil.
>
> [10]A river watering the garden flowed from Eden; from there it was separated into four headwaters. [11]The name of the first is the Pishon... [13]The name of the second river is the Gihon... [14]The name of the third river is the Tigris... And the fourth river is the Euphrates.

By transitioning to a specific location in verse 8, the author draws the audience into the central setting of the story—the garden of Eden. By further writing that God placed the man in the garden, the author conveys an image of the garden of Eden as bearing some significance to humankind and possibly to the God-human relationship. Then in verses 9 and 10 the author paints a verbal picture of the garden's importance. With its river supplying the four headwaters out of Eden, the garden of Eden is depicted as being on high ground and as being the primary source of water for the ancient Near Eastern world; the bountiful trees in the garden present a colorful palette of nourishment, and the Tree of Life offers a glimpse of eternal sustenance. With its water, food, and Tree of Life, the garden of Eden is portrayed as God's sustaining provision for humankind.

Later, in Genesis 2, we are told that Adam was to care for the garden and that God gave Adam this command:

> [16]And the LORD God commanded the man, "You are free to eat from any tree in the garden; [17]but you must not eat from the tree of the knowledge of good and evil, for when you eat of it you will surely die."

In the context of a utopian-esque creation story, verses 16 and 17 may seem out of place. They also beg a multitude of questions: why did God give the man freedom to eat from any tree in the garden but then prohibit the man from eating from the Tree of Knowledge of Good and Evil? For that matter, why did God even create this menacing tree? Why is death the consequence for eating the forbidden fruit?

In these two verses, it appears that God is seeking to establish a personal relationship with human beings by forming a bond of trust. You see, for a personal relationship to be genuine, you must have the freedom to choose between trust and distrust. Therefore, desiring that we trust him as the Sustainer of life, God presents humankind with a choice: trust God or trust self. Trust God by eating from the Tree of Life, or trust self by eating from the Tree of Knowledge of Good and Evil. The Tree of Life and the Tree of Knowledge of Good and Evil stand side by side at the center of the garden of Eden symbolizing the central question in the God-human personal relationship: "Do you trust me?"

Having drawn the audience into the central setting of the story, the author turns his attention to developing the plot.

Genesis 3 begins with Eve immersed in a conversation with a serpent. The serpent questions Eve about God's prohibition, and after Eve responds, the serpent proclaims, "You will not surely die, for God knows that when you eat of it your eyes will be opened, and you will be like God, knowing good and evil."

In the first five verses of chapter 3 we find an essential element of good storytelling—conflict. The serpent, playing the role of the antagonist, introduces tension among the characters in the garden of Eden: he instigates a man vs. nature conflict between Eve and himself by confronting Eve with God's prohibition, he initiates a nature vs. God conflict by indirectly accusing God of being a liar, he provokes a God vs. man conflict by casting doubt on whether God has humankind's best interest in mind, and he even stirs up a man-vs.-self conflict by presenting Eve with the dilemma of whom to trust.

In this garden of Eden drama, the conflict introduced at the start of Genesis 3 helps to develop the plot of whether humans should trust God. By suggesting that God is a liar and does not have humankind's best interest in mind, the serpent pushes Eve away from trusting God and toward eating from the Tree of Knowledge of Good and Evil. Faced with a dilemma, Eve must decide whether she should trust God, trust the serpent, or rely on her own understanding.

How will Eve answer the all-important question to the God-human personal relationship: "Do you trust me?"

Recognizing that our twenty-first-century world is not the garden of Eden, how do we today experience God's question: "Do you trust me?" What might it look like for us to trust God, and what might it mean for God to have our best interests in mind?

These are not merely abstract philosophical questions; they are relevant questions to the painful reality of living in a violent world. In the aftermath of earthquakes, tsunamis, hurricanes, tornadoes, floods, landslides, and other natural disasters you will find people searching for answers. What do you say when they ask, "If God is all-knowing, all-powerful, and all-loving, how could he have let this happen?"

The search to make sense of our brutal world is not confined to the debris of natural disasters. The devastating force of human depravity marks and mars every human civilization, reducing our communal existence to a wasteland of broken relationships and distrust. In the wreckage of our inhuman acts against one another you will find untold victims rummaging through their pain for answers.

To gain a sense of the overwhelming damage caused by depravity, stop for a moment and imagine you could see *every* human interaction within a one-mile radius of your residence over the past twenty-four hours. What kind of abuse and neglect would you see in just one day?

As disturbing as that thought might be, what if you could see all the horrors of human abuse and neglect throughout our global community? What if you could see the religious wars, ethnic clashes, murders, tortures, rapes, slavery, and child prostitution? What would you say to the countless victims? How would you answer their questions "Where was God?" "Why didn't God rescue me?" The response "You just need to trust God" will not appease their anger or console their pain. It sounds distant. It lacks compassion.

In a world flooded with tragedy and suffering, mere talk of an all-good, all-knowing, and all-powerful God does not calm our doubts about God or deepen our trust in God. Would telling my drowning daughter I could have helped sooner but had a better plan deepen her trust in me? From the opposite perspective, emerging theological positions that describe God as having limited his own influence or power in the world do not deepen trust in God either. Who wants to place trust in a God who is unable or unwilling to help us when we're in need?

Consciously or subconsciously most of us have experienced this dilemma of whether or not to trust God. Unless you've spent your life on an island, sheltered from pain, death, and disappointment, you've probably flailed in turbulent seas, asking yourself "Why should I trust God?" The unwanted and seemingly unjust events in life that push us to ask this question mirror the serpent's antagonistic allegations in Genesis 3. In response to being provoked, we humans instinctively struggle with whether to trust God; hence, the timeless brilliance of the garden of Eden drama in exposing the central conflict in the God-human personal relationship.

As long as the God-human relationship exists, as long as the ride lasts with God, there will be this essential, ever-present, unspoken question: "Do you trust me?"

I hope God is trustworthy.

I hope I answer, "Yes."

CHAPTER 2

≈

THE MERRYLESS-GO-ROUND

> When the woman saw that the fruit of the tree
> was good for food and pleasing to the eye, and also
> desirable for gaining wisdom, she took some and
> ate it. She also gave some to her husband, who was
> with her, and he ate it.
>
> —Genesis 3:6

LYING IN BED, I struggled to recall details from the previous night's escapade. My recollection of the evening began to turn hazy shortly after the girls quit nursing their wine coolers and we boys started playing "real" drinking games, where the last one standing would be declared the winner. In bed that next morning, I reveled in what I remembered of my exploits and lamented my lack of discretion, again.

Each of those mornings I would lie in a bed still spinning with my thoughts circling until I could create a story for my parents that included where I'd been, what I'd done, and when I'd come home. No one knew the severity of the problem, and I'm not referring to my alcohol abuse. The deeper issue was why I drank in the first place.

Nearly every moment of every day I felt the nerves you normally get right before taking a final exam or sharing a first kiss. Drinking melted the gnawing anxiety, and one binge released a week's worth of tension before the start of another week of trying to be perfect.

Truth be told, perfectionism was not the worst of my issues; I had a more disturbing problem. Funned out, I wanted to get off this ride, but no matter how loud I screamed, the ride never stopped. Despite my desperation I suppressed each passing thought of suicide. I couldn't subject my family and friends to that kind of pain—a numbing pain that could leave them emotionally paralyzed, a pain I knew well after a friend of mine had killed himself two years earlier. So instead I was a seventeen-year-old who held on with a death wish and a smile, hoping for an "accidental" out.

My life could have been one of those tragic stories you shake your head at in disbelief, wondering how it had happened—another reckless teenager wrapping his car around a telephone pole, leaving souls wrecked and voices questioning why "a kid who had everything going for him" would throw his life away.

Years passed before I began to understand my problem of wanting *more* out of life. My desire for more—more friends, more fun, more success, more money, more goods, more services, more everything, more anything—kept me yearning for more. Yet more was never enough, and regardless of how much more I achieved or acquired, the desire for more was never satisfied.

More than seventeen years have passed since then, but not much has changed. I'm still drawn by the allure of more and the occasional thought of an accidental out. The allure, though, has "matured" over the years. Vocational accomplishments, home repairs, retirement funds, and quality time with the wife and kids are sophisticated replacements for the grades, goals, and girls of my teen years.

To be clear, I'm not suggesting that success at work, nice things, and spending time with family are somehow wrong; what I'm saying is that more of something will never make me happy, satisfied, or complete. The allure of more cannot be appeased regardless of how much more I acquire or how noble the more might be.

I do not suffer alone. The allure of more is epidemic in American society. More work promises more money and more recognition. More credit cards permit the purchase of more stuff. More creatively structured loans allow for more house and more car. More cosmetic surgery portrays more youth. More divorces stimulate more personal fulfillment. And more sleep deprivation provides more time to pursue more of everything else.

We can go to bed at night hoping our world will stop spinning before we awake, but morning eventually ushers in an end to our dreams. Like clockwork we get out of bed to ring-a-ling music, feigning contentment for at least one more day of whirling on this tedious ride. Why don't we see the ride for what it is—a circling pursuit for more that keeps us unsettled, frustrated, and medicating our senses to avoid reality?

As we continue to circle, afraid of the uncertainty that would come with letting go and jumping into the unknown, we hold on with the hope that the ride will someday, somehow, slow to a stop. Unfortunately, we'll likely keep on riding, riding, riding the merryless-go-round, for it started spinning long ago, and there is no apparent end in sight.

How would you like to have a full-time job that required you to work only twenty-two hours per week? Or instead, how about a job that included twenty-five weeks of paid vacation per year? Or how about the possibility of retiring at age thirty-eight? Economist Dr. Juanita Kreps testified before a Unites States Senate committee that these possibilities could be a reality within seventeen years.[2] But before we get our hopes too high, I should reveal that Dr. Kreps gave this testimony to the Senate committee in 1967!

More than forty years have passed since Dr. Kreps's testimony, and the merryless-go-round has yet to slow down. In fact, our dizzying spin continues to pick up speed in the twenty-first century, leaving us to wonder whatever happened to the possibility of less work and earlier retirement.

To provide some context to Dr. Kreps's projections, her testimony came before a Senate Special Committee on Aging, formed in compliance with a Senate resolution to study "any and all matters pertaining to problems and opportunities of older people."[3] Although the committee focused primarily on issues related to the elderly, its report also included a chapter that addressed the projected imminent and significant increase in the number of retirees. It was theorized that the convergence of three factors—the number of Americans reaching age sixty-five, increasing life spans, and decreasing work life—would result in a "retirement revolution."

Seymour Wolfbein, former director of federal manpower programs, testified that since World War II the average work life had decreased at a rate of 3 percent per year and that "increased productivity is almost certain to result in further reductions of the labor force needed by industries and farms, and more Americans will find that they have free time on their hands."[4] It was in the context of establishing the potential extent of this new free time that Dr. Kreps gave her testimony.

In addition to sharing her research data and projections, Dr. Kreps offered suggestions for how the Senate could possibly ease the rate and magnitude of the "retirement revolution." A few of her ideas included lengthening education periods, offering sabbaticals to blue-collar workers, and reducing the traditional retirement age from sixty-five to sixty. Yet in the end Dr. Kreps conceded that "major social readjustments" would be needed regardless of what legislation was passed to curb the effects of increased productivity. In other words, Dr. Kreps concluded that society would inevitably have to deal with the impending issue of more Americans having more free time.

Today, some forty-five years later, let me ask you: how often do you find yourself sitting around doing nothing, thinking "I have so much free time I just don't know what to do with myself"? Could you imagine the government having acted on the Senate's report by forming a Department of Social Readjustment? What would those government programs have been like?

In twenty-first-century America we no longer conceptualize free time as an abundant commodity that new technologies will continue to discover and refine. As with crude oil, we're finding that time is a limited resource that increases in value as its supply is consumed by our insatiable addiction for more. Unfortunately, unlike its ability to offer us alternative forms of energy, technology doesn't currently offer us alternative forms of time. When it comes to acquiring more free time, the best technology has to offer is an alarm clock to help us get an earlier start on our day.

It was not supposed to work out this way. Technological advances were supposed to make our lives easier, not busier. What happened? How did we get here? And how do we get off the merryless-go-round?

When we left the garden of Eden drama, Eve had just been doused by the serpent's wave of accusations that God was a liar and that God did not have her best interest in mind. Overwhelmed with doubt, Eve was left to answer the all-important question in the God-human personal relationship: "Do you trust me?" How did she respond? Did Eve choose to eat from the Tree of Knowledge of Good and Evil, or did she forgo the forbidden fruit?

In evaluating the situation, Eve looked at the Tree of Knowledge of Good and Evil and saw that "the fruit of the tree was good for food and pleasing to the eye." To Eve the fruit did not appear deadly, dangerous, or even suspicious. The fruit on the tree looked "good for food," just like the fruit on every other fruit-bearing tree in the garden.

It is at this point in the drama that you can imagine Eve asking herself the question "Why not?" If the fruit on the Tree of Knowledge of Good and Evil is good for food and pleasing to the eye, why not eat it? Drawn by the appeal of the forbidden fruit, Eve was experiencing temptation—an allure that would test her trust in God. The temptation to eat, however, did not in itself violate her relationship with God. It is only when temptation gives birth to mental or physical action that the cord of trust is cut.

Eve then deduced that the fruit would be "desirable for gaining wisdom." In that she had her answer. Seeing that the fruit from the Tree of Knowledge of Good and Evil was good for food, pleasing to the eye, and desirable for gaining wisdom, she "took some and ate it. She also gave some to her husband, who was with her, and he ate it."

The moment Eve and Adam ate the forbidden fruit, the trust relationship between each of them and God was severed. By choosing to do what seemed right in their own eyes, they seized control of the situation, declaring their independence from God. With no more rules or regulations to follow, Adam and Eve were flying high on the merryless-go-round, enjoying the thrill of eating forbidden fruit.

For us, living in twenty-first-century America, how do the actions of Adam and Eve translate to our experience? Given that we don't have access to either the Tree of Knowledge of Good and Evil or any of its fruit, how do we answer the all-important question in the God-human personal relationship, "Do you trust me?"

Before contextualizing the account of Adam and Eve to our lives, let's consider the influence the children's version of the story has had on our perception of the forbidden fruit and our understanding of the drama.

If you were raised in the United States, you probably heard about Adam and Eve eating the forbidden fruit at least once during your childhood. If you're anything like me, the children's version of the story acquired a fairy-tale-like mystique, happening once upon a time, long ago, in a faraway place, with the serpent plotting to eliminate the naïve maiden, and the forbidden fruit—the serpent's agent of death—taking on the shrouded identity of a spellbound apple. In this fairy-tale rendering the garden of Eden drama is reduced to a moral lesson on the need to obey God or else.

The children's version of the Adam and Eve story is so prevalent and accepted in our culture that when I speak on the subject, most people are surprised to hear that the biblical account does not state that the forbidden fruit was an apple. In fact, the type of fruit Adam and Eve ate is not revealed anywhere in the Bible. To take it a step further, to my knowledge there is no definitive historical record or consensus identifying the kind of fruit Adam and Eve ate, but the perception that the forbidden fruit was an apple has been so accepted in our society that it has reached the status of common knowledge.

What other inaccuracies might we have accepted as common knowledge or truth from our children's version of the story, and how might they have affected our understanding of the account?

In the teaching of the Adam and Eve story, there has been a long-standing and widely held assumption that the forbidden fruit contained extraordinary properties (either physical, spiritual, mystical, or magical) that differentiated it from all other fruit in the garden of Eden. Believing that this fruit was in some fashion pregnant with the knowledge of good and evil, scholars have theorized that by consuming the forbidden fruit humankind would acquire a knowledge that once obtained would lead to death. These presumptions have resulted in the generally accepted teaching that God's prohibition was an act of love to protect humankind from the lethal effects of the forbidden fruit.

However, the story does not state—directly or even indirectly— that the fruit from the Tree of Knowledge of Good and Evil possessed any distinctive properties whatsoever. On the contrary, based on the portrait of the garden of Eden painted in Genesis 2, the Tree of Knowledge of Good and Evil was created along with the Tree of Life and every other fruit-bearing tree in the garden of Eden—all of which are described in Genesis 2:8–9 as being good for food and pleasing to the eye. Additionally, in God's command to Adam, "You must not eat from the tree of the knowledge of good and evil, for when you eat of it you will surely die," there is no indication of how, when, or why death would occur. The accepted position that the essence of the forbidden fruit was somehow different from the other fruit in the garden is at best speculation but more likely a misrepresentation of the story, wrongly portraying the Tree of Knowledge of Good and Evil and its fruit as the source of death.

The lack of clarity surrounding the forbidden fruit's identity and its connection to the knowledge of good and evil is somewhat puzzling. Arguably it's the most important piece of fruit in the story of humankind and we don't even know what it was, let alone whether it contained forbidden knowledge. Why?

I've come to believe that the original storyteller did not reveal the fruit's identity because the fruit itself is not that important to the story. Identifying the fruit might have even been a distraction, directing the audience's attention away from the participants in the drama and onto the fruit itself. If the author had revealed the type of fruit that hung on the Tree of Knowledge of Good and Evil, then maybe humans would have cut down and burned every such "evil" tree just as we have cut down and burned "evil" books and "evil" people, thinking that the problem of evil in the world could be eradicated by destroying "evil" forms.

Good and evil, however, are not determined by form but rather by function. For example, a gun is often viewed as an evil form, while a Bible is often viewed as a good form. But guns and Bibles are amoral—neither inherently good nor inherently evil. A gun can be used with good intentions, while a Bible can be used with evil intentions. What determines the goodness or evilness of a form is the function for which it is used.

There is a significant difference between questioning a form and questioning its function. When we question a form, we can make the mistake of casting judgment on that form when the problem is really a matter of how and why that form is used.

With respect to the forbidden fruit in the garden of Eden, we have been asking the form question *"What* did Adam and Eve eat?" rather than the function question *"Why* did Adam and Eve eat?" The form question questions the integrity of the fruit, whereas the function question questions the integrity of humankind. By focusing on form over function, we allow ourselves to blame a form instead of taking responsibility for our own motives and actions.

When it comes to the garden of Eden drama, the story is told in a fashion that frames the function question more than the form question. If the story had been about what Adam and Eve had eaten, then you'd think the author would have given more time to describing the Tree of Knowledge of Good and Evil and its fruit. Instead, the drama is framed in a relational manner that should lead the audience to ask why Adam and Eve chose to distrust God by eating the forbidden fruit.

With the function question "Why?" in mind, let's return to Eve's observations in verse 6 to see why Adam and Eve ate the forbidden fruit.

Eve saw that "the fruit of the tree was good for food and pleasing to the eye, and also desirable for gaining wisdom." Because the fruit of all the trees in the garden of Eden was good for food, we should not be surprised that Eve saw the forbidden fruit as being good for food. Additionally, we should not be surprised by Eve questioning why she should not eat it.

Like Eve, don't we all sometimes ask why not? It seems as though every time I tell my oldest daughter "No, you can't," she asks "Why not?" Frankly, the apple doesn't fall far from the tree. Whenever I walk through a hospital, I pass countless closed doors without a second thought. Yet as soon as I see a door with the placard "Authorized Personnel Only," I become "that guy" wondering defiantly *Why not? Why am I not allowed in that room?* When the reason behind a prohibition is not obvious or explained, don't you sometimes ask, "Why not?"

When we ask that why not question and are not given a satisfying answer, we examine the facts of the situation. In Eve's case, she worked with three facts: the fruit was good for food, the fruit was pleasing to the eye, and the fruit would provide wisdom. In other words, as Eve saw it, the forbidden fruit was edible, desirable, and beneficial. Relying on her own understanding, Eve made the logical deduction that God must have forbidden humankind from eating this perfectly good fruit because he did not want humans "to be like God, knowing good and evil," just as the serpent had said. Therefore, believing that God was withholding something good, Eve concluded that God was not trustworthy, and she did what was right in her own eyes—"she took some and ate it. She also gave some to her husband, who was with her, and he ate it."

Looking now to our experience, do you ever do what seems right in your own eyes? Regardless of what rules are in place, do you ever evaluate the facts of a situation and after doing so choose to break the rules? As an individualistically minded society, are we not taught to look out for our own best interests? As Americans, are we not taught that we have the God-given right to life, liberty, and the pursuit of happiness? Why are we surprised when government officials, corporate executives, or religious leaders break the law or betray our trust in pursuit of their own happiness? Why are we surprised that the rich want to pay less in taxes and the poor want to receive more in social services? Are we not all biased toward our self-interests? Don't we all at times do what seems right in our own eyes regardless of what laws we break or relationships we violate? Don't we all at times want what we want when we want it and then justify and rationalize our self-centered acts?

There didn't need to be anything extraordinary about the Tree of Knowledge of Good and Evil or its fruit because the story is not about *what* Eve and Adam ate, or about an evil *form*, or about a moral lesson on the need to obey God or else. The story of Adam and Eve is the human story of our determining for ourselves what is good and evil and in doing so attempting to sustain our own existence.

Although we don't have the choice between eating from the Tree of Life and the Tree of Knowledge of Good and Evil, each of us in our own way examines the forbidden fruit, asking why we should not eat it. Each of us in our own way struggles with the question "Do you trust me?" Sometimes we overcome the temptation to do what seems right in our own eyes, but other times the allure of more, offering a delightful illusion of control and satisfaction, proves too much to suppress, and we indulge ourselves with the forbidden fruit.

As we mature, the merryless-go-round can lose its thrill, and at times we might even lament our lack of discretion and wish that we'd never climbed onboard. Yet our obsession with control keeps us from letting go and jumping into the unknown.

As we continue to circle round and round, we hold on with the hope that the ride will someday, somehow, slow to a stop. Unfortunately, as long as we continue eating forbidden fruit, we will continue riding the merryless-go-round, for it started spinning long ago, and there is no apparent end in sight.

CHAPTER 3

≈

MANNEQUINS ON DISPLAY

⁷Then the eyes of both of them were opened, and they realized they were naked; so they sewed fig leaves together and made coverings for themselves.

⁸Then the man and his wife heard the sound of the LORD God as he was walking in the garden in the cool of the day, and they hid from the LORD God among the trees of the garden. ⁹But the LORD God called to the man, "Where are you?"

¹⁰ He answered, "I heard you in the garden, and I was afraid because I was naked; so I hid."

—Genesis 3:7–10

HAVE YOU EVER had a dream of being seen naked in public? As a child, I used to have this recurring dream of standing in line to buy lunch in my elementary school cafeteria only to look down and realize I'd forgotten to get dressed that morning. Overwhelmed with shame, I'd just stand there, helplessly vulnerable, asking myself, *Will anyone notice I'm naked?* With nowhere to run and desperate to gain control of the situation, I'd wake up from the nightmare.

Slowly, relief would spread through my being as I discovered it had been just a bad dream.

The fear of being seen naked is often more than a bad dream. The following story is one of those childhood experiences I'd like to remember in greater detail but then again I'd also like to forget entirely. Recalling this memory is like flipping through an envelope of old photographs that never found their way into an album. I open the envelope with nervous anticipation, wondering what treasures lie inside waiting to be relived. The photographs tell a story that transcends words not because the pictures themselves are that valuable but because mental photos tell a story that neither words nor pictures can ever capture in full.

The colors in this particular roll of mental photographs have remained crisp. The first photo is of a fire-engine-red pellet dispenser at the edge of a pond that contains brown morsels for feeding ducks. The second photo is of a silver quarter, lying in the palm of a small hand, reflecting the light of the sun. The third photo is of the same hand, cupped and full of happy pills for the ducks.

I remember standing on the concrete deck at the water's edge, reaching out my hand to feed my new friends. As I was feeding them, an enormous white duck swam up to me. I was old enough to capture this mental photo, but I wasn't old enough to know that if you were flipping through my photos you'd call this enormous white duck a swan. The swan had no interest in consuming duck pellets, so as I reached out my hand, my betrayer began to backpedal.

I'd like to write that I then turned around and ran to my mother crying for her affection because a big white "duck" was rejecting me. That's what I'd like to write, but I can't; my mental pictures tell a different story.

I'm a rather persistent person. I always have been. So as the swan continued to retreat, I continued to lean forward. As gravity was about to teach me a very important lesson, my entire being began to scream, "This is not good!"

The next photo was taken underwater.

As I look at this underwater shot I'm reminded of my frail humanity. The picture is dark—very dark. To you it's just a black image captured by someone who forgot to remove the lens cap, but to me it's a snapshot revealing the terror and despair of a child too scared to open his eyes, vividly seeing his life on the brink. I never like looking at this picture or any other one like it. The black void often recalls memories I'd rather forget. Other times it elicits fearful thoughts of death and eternal nothingness.

Now if the final photo in this rediscovered roll were a downward shot of a small body in sopping wet clothes, this treasure would not be the find that it is. No. This is the envelope of pictures that makes cleaning out your attic worth it… at least for everyone else who catches a glimpse of the priceless cache.

Before going any further, I pause to note that my mother is from "the old country," a simple, nondescript reference to any community outside the United States (but most likely a remote village somewhere in Europe). When a person is identified as being from the old country, the expression is often used as a respectful disclaimer to explain and excuse beliefs and customs most Americans would consider foreign and possibly even objectionable.

My mother, being from the old country, has the cultural belief that you'll likely get sick if you wear wet clothes. So after fishing me out of the water, my mother sought to get my clothes dry as quickly as possible. She took me to a spot where we'd have direct sunlight and a breeze. As my mental photo reveals, that location was the apex of a white pedestrian bridge set against a blue sky.

When we got there, my mother removed my clothes—every piece—and draped them, along with my dignity, over the railing. I can still see them hanging there. The mental photo of listlessness ushers in a most uncomfortable angst. Everyone would see my nakedness.

Just when you thought the roll of pictures was done, there are a few bonus exposures. To cover my shame and any dignity that may not have been draped over the railing, my mother transformed her scarf into a diaper-like garment. Unfortunately for me, the scarf my mother chose to wear that day was a summer scarf—colorful and translucent. So instead of my shame being covered, my shame was displayed like a neon sign for all to see. My mother still has that scarf, and I can hear it snicker every time we meet.

The last shots on this roll of mental photos are a sequence of pictures of two women passing by as we waited for the sun and the breeze to perform their painfully slow magic. As I now look at the two women, each with hand over mouth in the last photo, I want to give the disclaimer that my mother is from the old country, yet even with the disclaimer I know I still feel naked and ashamed.

⁓

What is your greatest fear? Some researchers tell us our greatest fear is public speaking. Yet when you think about it, the fear of public speaking isn't a fear of being in public or a fear of speaking, it's a fear of making a mistake or not having an answer to a question. We fear being laughed at. We fear whispering words. We fear judgment. We fear being seen naked.

The fear of being seen naked runs much deeper than simply a fear of being found without clothes. It's a fear that a suit of armor can't cover—a fear we live with every day. Imagine if in an instant every thought you've ever had and everything you've ever said and done were fully exposed for all to see. How would you feel? Naked?

In response, we are consumed with covering and hiding the truth of who we are, what we think, and the shameful things we've said and done. We pretend to be smarter, stronger, purer, more beautiful, and better in countless other ways than we really are. We're desperately afraid of being seen naked.

To mask our fear we spend our lives in disguise. Like mannequins on display, we change our clothes to the latest fashions, we fix our hair to the newest styles, and we display ourselves with plastic smiles, hoping that all who pass by will like what they see.

The truth, of course, is that we are not mannequins. We are not filled with foam; we're filled with other stuff that makes us human, and not simply the blood and guts stuff. There are aspects of our humanity that cannot be contained in a box or measured on a scale. Passion and emotion flood and flow from our bodies. Passion and emotion are what inspire us to experience our humanity. Mannequins don't feel the shame of being laughed at or the pain of cancer or the sadness of death. And mannequins don't feel the joy, wonder, and love that come with being human.

I don't want to live like a mannequin on display with a lifeless smile, void of inner consciousness and feeling, but I don't want to be seen naked. When seen naked I often feel vulnerable, weak, and insecure. This creates a particularly difficult dilemma because as an American I'm supposed to be confident, strong, and invincible. I cannot be seen naked—it's … it's un-American!

So then what should I do? What should we do? How do we stop living like mannequins on display?

━

The last we saw of Adam and Eve, they were in the garden of Eden, eating from the Tree of Knowledge of Good and Evil. In eating the forbidden fruit, they were declaring their independence from God. No longer trusting God as the Sustainer of life, they were free to sustain themselves and live as they pleased.

"Then the eyes of both of them were opened, and they realized they were naked; so they sewed fig leaves together and made coverings for themselves." After eating the forbidden fruit, Adam and Eve saw themselves as being naked. Their realization that they were naked has been and still is interpreted in various ways.

Viewing the story from a historical perspective, Hebraic tradition teaches that prior to eating the forbidden fruit, Adam and Eve were clothed with the light of God's glory. To be clothed in God's light meant that a being literally radiated God's holy glow.

Hebrew Scriptures contain numerous stories regarding God's glory and how humans were afraid to look upon its various manifestations. The Scriptures tell us that when Moses came down from Mount Sinai with the Ten Commandments, his face was radiant because he had spoken with God. The Israelites were so struck with fear when they saw Moses come down that after he gave them God's commandments he put a veil over his face. Thereafter, Moses would remove the veil before each meeting with God, and then after each meeting he would put the veil back over his face to ease the Israelites' fears. Such a display of godly radiance was an indication of one's having a close, personal relationship with God. In the case of Adam and Eve, their radiance would have signified their authoritative position as God's ruling agents over the earth.

If for argument's sake Adam and Eve were clothed with God's glory, then their eating from the Tree of Knowledge of Good and Evil would have undermined their personal relationship with God. No longer submitting themselves to God, Adam and Eve could have lost God's radiance as a natural consequence of their action. The forbidden fruit did not need to contain anti-glow or any deglorifying properties. The very act of eating the fruit would have broken the God-human personal relationship, resulting in Adam and Eve forfeiting their role as God's radiating agents on earth.

Most other interpretations of "the eyes of both of them were opened" and "they realized they were naked" teach that Adam and Eve experienced some form of self-realization. One common interpretation is that in eating the forbidden fruit Adam and Eve became self-aware or self-conscious and therefore noticed their nakedness for the first time. A second interpretation is that eating the forbidden fruit caused Adam and Eve to shift their primary attention from God onto themselves, resulting in their becoming self-absorbed and therefore feeling insecure with their nakedness. Yet another interpretation is the "innocence lost" position, which argues that in eating from the Tree of Knowledge of Good and Evil, Adam and Eve lost a childlike innocence. Among those who hold the innocence-lost position, there's a difference of opinion as to the nature of the innocence lost. Some suggest that Adam and Eve lost a sense of naïve bliss, while others argue that losing their innocence meant they'd gained an understanding of their sexuality, and still others offer different nuances for the childlike innocence Adam and Eve lost. In short, there's a general lack of agreement over what occurred the moment "the eyes of both them were opened and they realized they were naked."

For our purposes, however, knowing what happened the moment their eyes were opened is not crucial. The important observation for us is what Adam and Eve did in response to seeing themselves naked: "they sewed fig leaves together and made coverings for themselves."

Adam and Eve responded to the realization of their nakedness by covering themselves with fig leaves. The Hebrew text could be more specifically translated that they covered their genitalia. Whatever they covered, the point is that they chose to cover part(s) of their bodies. This observation is important because the preceding chapter ends with the words "The man and his wife were both naked, and they felt no shame." Before the Genesis 3 story even begins, the audience's attention has been drawn to the fact that Adam and Eve were naked and unashamed. Adam and Eve's realization that they were naked was a revelation to them but not to the audience. From our vantage point they had been naked from the beginning; their physical nakedness is not new to the story. What is new is that in seeing their nakedness they felt shame. As recipients of the story we're being directed to notice that after eating the fruit from the Tree of Knowledge of God and Evil Adam and Eve were feeling both naked and ashamed.

Outside the fullness of the garden of Eden drama, it is understandable that one would read Genesis 3 and focus on just the nakedness of Adam and Eve, which is why a common application from the account is the importance of modesty. Yet within the context of the entire story the point of emphasis is that only after eating the forbidden fruit did Adam and Eve covered their naked bodies in an effort to mask their shame.

Have you ever done what seemed right in your own eyes and then sometime afterward felt ashamed? Shame typically surfaces when someone confronts us with our misdeeds, when doing what seems right in our own eyes results in unexpected or unwanted consequences, or when the stirring of guilt becomes too much to suppress. As long as we don't feel too guilty and as long as what we're doing is "working," we enjoy the ride on the merryless-go-round. It's only when doing what seems right in our own eyes is threatened or stops working that we begin to realize the merryless-go-round may not be the endless joyride we once thought it would be.

As for Adam and Eve, we don't know whether they felt guilty after eating the forbidden fruit or whether they experienced some unexpected or unwanted consequence. We can, though, deduce that eating the fruit did not work as they'd intended because they responded by trying to cover their shame.

Like Adam and Eve, when doing what seems right in our own eyes is threatened or ceases to work, we try to cover our shame. We try to protect and preserve ourselves by covering the truth of what we've done. When children play ball in the house and break Mom's favorite vase, they try to glue the broken pieces back together before she finds out. Teenagers chew gum, squirt eyedrops, and splash on fragrances to try to cover the evidence of their misdeeds. And adults know how to manipulate the facts and lie to cover the shameful things they've done.

After Adam and Eve covered themselves with fig leaves, Genesis 3:8 tells us, "Then the man and his wife heard the sound of the LORD God as he was walking in the garden in the cool of the day, and they hid from the LORD God among the trees of the garden." Adam and Eve hid when they heard God coming because they knew their efforts to cover their shame would be insufficient before God.

When we don't have enough time or are unable to cover our shame, we hide. When children hear footsteps after breaking Mom's favorite vase, they run to their favorite place to hide. When teenagers don't have time to mask their wrongdoings, they find someplace to hide. And adults, with a lifetime of experience dealing with shame, have plenty of places to hide.

While Adam and Eve were hiding from God among the trees in the garden, verse 9 tells us, "the LORD God called to the man, 'Where are you?'"

When you think about it, God calling out "Where are you?" is not all that different from a parent following a trail of crumbs from a cookie jar to a bedroom closet, calling out to a child, "Where are you?" This calling out is not so much a question as it is an invitation. God's asking "Where are you?" was an invitation for Adam to come out of hiding and confess what he'd done. God was giving Adam the opportunity to admit he'd eaten the forbidden fruit, much like a parent calling out to a child, giving him or her the opportunity to admit to eating the forbidden cookie. The invitation to come out of hiding and tell the truth is an opportunity to begin restoring a personal relationship that has been violated by an act of distrust.

How do we respond to an invitation to come out of hiding? Here's how Adam responded to God: "He answered, 'I heard you in the garden, and I was afraid because I was naked; so I hid.'" Adam's answer was an odd response. Rather than confessing to having eaten from the Tree of Knowledge of Good and Evil, Adam told God he'd hid because he was naked. What makes Adam's response particularly odd is that he was no longer naked; Adam and Eve had already clothed themselves with fig leaves prior to hiding among the trees in the garden.

Was Adam lying about being naked, or was there more to Adam's nakedness than meets the eye?

If you look carefully at Adam's response, you'll see that Adam didn't simply say he was naked; he said he was *afraid* because he was naked. Fear is an emotion we experience when we sense life spinning out of control. When God called out to Adam, "Where are you?" Adam could sense that he was losing control of the situation, and he was afraid of being seen naked.

You see, the fear of being seen naked is more than a fear of being seen without clothes; it's a fear of being exposed. Whenever some aspect of our being we want to keep secret—a part of our bodies, a thought we have, or something we've said or done—is revealed, we feel naked. The feeling of nakedness is an emotional response to the unnerving realization that some detail of our lives has been made public, and we are left standing out in the open, unable to control the reactions or responses of those who catch a glimpse of our naked truth. We don't like to be seen naked; it exposes our insecurities, our flawed humanity, and our inability to sustain ourselves forever. Nothing threatens the illusion of being in control more than standing stark naked in front of another human being or God. Nothing.

Desperate to maintain control of a situation, we do anything we can to cover and hide the truth in order to avoid the shame of being seen naked. We cover and hide in an attempt to protect and preserve ourselves and to regain a sense of satisfaction on the merryless-go round.

It's only a matter of time, though, before the merryless-go-round starts to lose its thrill. Eventually, doing what seems right in our own eyes results in unwanted consequences, or we are confronted with the truth, or the guilt becomes too much to bear. But instead of jumping off the merryless-go-round and allowing the consequences of the truth to take their due course, we continue to protect and preserve self by covering and hiding. Even when given an invitation to come out of hiding, we often prefer to hold on by deflecting the truth in hopes of preserving the illusion of being in control.

The instinctive desire to protect and preserve self is what inspires us to live like mannequins on display, covering and hiding the truth of who we are, what we think, and the shameful things we've said and done. That's why we pretend to be smarter, stronger, purer, more beautiful, and better in countless other ways than we really are. We don't want to be naked—we don't want to expose our vulnerability or see our mortality. What we want is to believe that we're in control of our lives and that we can somehow sustain ourselves forever. To these ends we spend billions of dollars each year trying to preserve our mannequin veneers.

As I get older, I see more and more of how I'm becoming "that guy" who stares in the mirror at his receding hairline. I thought the aging process would gently guide me through adolescent vanity. Instead, aging is starting to expose the depths of my vanity. I don't like going bald, and I don't consider my love handles to be lovely at all. I now feel insecure in ways I never did years ago. Insecurities I never knew were there have become visible as the signs of aging disfigure my veneer and reveal my mortality.

Unfortunately, our veneers are not composed of our mere cosmetic appearances. We cover and hide every aspect of our existence that might cause us to feel weak, vulnerable, or out of control. Those who find security in their intellects want to be seen as the smartest kids in class. Those who find strength in their athletic ability grapple with the limitations that come with aging. Those who seek control through financial security obsess over whether they have enough money. Those who seek to impress with worldly possessions need to show off their newest acquisitions. And those who crave the approval of others tailor themselves to appeal to each person who passes by.

You may never have had a dream of being seen naked in public or have experienced the nightmare of wearing nothing but your mother's translucent scarf, but I'm sure you know the fear of being exposed. In response to fear we use any means possible to gain control of the situation. If we don't have the power or authority to seize control, we cover and hide the truth. We live like mannequins on display—each of us in our own way covering and hiding our shame to protect and preserve self.

The naked truth is that we like doing what seems right in our own eyes, we like the illusion of being in control, and we like the delusion that we can sustain our own existence. Unless we acknowledge and change the way we see ourselves in this world, we'll simply continue to cover the naked truth by living like mannequins on display.

CHAPTER 4

~

THE BLAME GAME

¹¹And he said, "Who told you that you were naked? Have you eaten from the tree that I commanded you not to eat from?"

¹²The man said, "The woman you put here with me—she gave me some fruit from the tree, and I ate it."

¹³Then the LORD God said to the woman, "What is this you have done?"

The woman said, "The serpent deceived me, and I ate."

—Genesis 3:11–13

DURING THE SUMMER between sixth and seventh grades, I started hanging out with this kid named Danny. He and I knew each other from middle school, but you wouldn't say we were friends. Danny was not the type to make friends at school; he was too busy getting in trouble. He sassed teachers, got into fights, and spent a whole lot of time in in-school suspension. Come to think of it, I have no idea what led to our friendship that summer.

Anyway, Danny and I started spending a lot of time together, so much so that one afternoon we made plans for him to stay for dinner and sleep over. After dinner, Danny and I walked to a convenience store down the road from my house. While we were in the store, Danny suggested we buy a can of WD-40 and light fires. I had no idea what he was talking about. He explained that WD-40 was a flammable liquid we could spray on things and light on fire.

Like any "normal" twelve-year-old boy, my mind went through the following sequence of thoughts: 1. Do what? 2. Light fires? 3. We could get in trouble. 4. I like fire. 5. Okay.

Danny picked up a can of WD-40, grabbed a couple packs of matches off the checkout counter, and paid the cashier. In hindsight, why a cashier would allow children to make such a purchase is beyond me. She might as well have handed us a complementary brochure on how to start fires with household products.

Anyway, dusk was approaching, and we needed a plan. Danny and I decided to walk to the elementary school about a half-mile down the road. When we got there, Danny sprayed some WD-40 on the blacktop and lit it. It was actually pretty cool. Eventually we moved our way up to the redbrick walls of the school.

After a while we started to get bored, so we began looking for other stuff to burn. As we rounded a corner of the school, I saw a custodian in the parking lot hunched over and talking into a car window. Before I could figure out what was happening, sirens started blaring, lights started flashing, and the car hopped the curb and began tearing toward us.

Scared out of my mind, I did what any "normal" twelve-year-old boy would do: I yelled "Cops!" and ran for my life.

Danny ran too, but he was a husky kid—neither fast nor fit. So not long into our getaway Danny gave himself up. I on the other hand had no intention of stopping. I dashed around the front of the school, ran down a side street, and hid behind a car.

As I squatted behind the car with my heart racing, the bleak reality of the situation began to set in. As though it hadn't been bad enough that Danny had gotten caught, I had no idea what to tell my mother. What was I going to say when she asked me, "Where's Danny?" I certainly couldn't play dumb by answering, "Huh? I don't know. I guess he must have walked home." So I sat behind the car until the darkness of night covered me, wondering what story to tell my mother.

Finally I got up and started to walk home, hoping that the cop had let Danny go and that I'd find him on the way to my house. Instead, just as I approached the school, the police car drove off the lawn, right in front of me. The vehicle stopped, the driver's window rolled down, and the officer asked me where I was coming from and where I was going. I was not remotely ready to answer his questions; I'd been thinking about how to respond to my mother's questions. Caught off guard, I started babbling about coming home from an ice cream shop up the road. (Yeah, right—a twelve-year-old walking home, alone, in the dark, from an ice cream shop a mile away.) Thinking about how to salvage my lame lie, I caught a glimpse of Danny in the back seat. Under the dim light of the car's dome Danny was silently mouthing to me, "Don't lie. Don't lie." At that point I knew I was done, so I told the truth.

The police officer got out of the car, opened the back door, and sat me inside. I looked at Danny. He just sat there with a pathetic look on his face, a stray dog on his way to the pound. I knew this wasn't Danny's first time in a police car. I was furious with him for getting me into this mess and for his inability to run away. The officer got back into the driver's seat and began asking me the standard battery of personal questions: name, address, height, weight, eye color, and so on. Then he began asking me about the events of that evening.

After I finished telling him what had happened, the officer explained that what we had been doing was very dangerous and that we could have lit the school on fire. At the time I didn't realize the officer was trying to scare us straight; I was still too angry about being in this mess. So when the officer was explaining the great damage we could have caused, I didn't cry, apologize, or even thank him for informing me about the dangers of fire. No. Instead, I questioned him. I asked him how the school could catch on fire—it was made of brick. He then stated that the heat of the flames could penetrate the brick and start a fire inside the building. Again, instead of crying or apologizing for my behavior, I scoffed at his explanation and said something like, "That's impossible." After my less-than-contrite response, the officer took a different approach; he asked me for directions to my house.

When we pulled up to the house, the officer got out and told us to stay inside the car. I watched him walk to the front door and ring the doorbell. The door opened in slow motion, and there stood my mother. That's when fear really took hold of me. The officer and my mother began talking, and he turned and pointed to us in the car. My mother stepped outside, and the officer escorted her down the driveway.

When they reached the car, the officer opened the back door and asked us to step out. He released us into the custody of my mother. He said something to Danny and me, but I don't remember what it was; I was more concerned about what my mother was going to say.

She didn't say a word until we got into the house. Once inside, she said, "Go to bed." That was all she said, but that was not all she was saying. Mothers have the remarkable capacity to communicate with their eyes. I heard "Go to bed," but I saw volumes of disgust and disappointment.

The next morning my mother took Danny home. When she returned, we had a talk. She asked me about what had happened the previous night. Not long into the story my mother started asking questions: "So it was Danny's idea to go to the store? It was Danny's idea to light fires?"

Unlike in my conversation with the police officer, I quickly figured out where this talk was going. My mother was giving me the opportunity to blame the whole fiasco on Danny. And that's exactly what I did.

My mother lectured me about the importance of choosing friends wisely. She went down the "I told you so" road, explaining again why I shouldn't spend time with kids like Danny. I told her that she was right, that I should have listened to her from the beginning. The talk ended with my mother forbidding me from being friends with Danny and telling me he was never allowed to come to our house again.

That was it. There was no court appearance or three- to five-year sentence for disorderly conduct. No probation. No punishment. No nothing.

As I look back to that summer between sixth and seventh grades, I realize that my short-lived friendship with Danny taught me an important lesson about life: if you want to play with fire and not get burned, you have to be committed to playing the blame game.

~

You know the blame game. It's the game people play when they don't want to take responsibility for their actions. It's the game professional athletes play when the news breaks that they used performance-enhancing drugs, and it's the game politicians play to get elected and later to explain away their broken promises.

To be fair, public figures aren't the only people who play the blame game. You'll find children playing it in daycare centers and seniors playing it in nursing homes. Coworkers play it at the office, friends play it at the mall, and families play it around the dinner table. Whether it's in person, on the phone, or over the Internet, people play the blame game all around us all the time. And, if we take an honest look at ourselves—you and I—we'll see that we play the blame game too.

The blame game is simple to play. There's no game board, and there are no pieces to worry about. There is no limit to the number of players—anywhere from two people to millions can play. And there are no rules to follow. In fact, lying, cheating, and stealing are not only allowed, they are essential elements of the game.

As for how to start a game, most begin when people are unexpectedly confronted with something they've thought, said, or done. At that point a person can either accept responsibility or respond by blaming someone or something else. If the person chooses the blame option, then a game has officially begun.

In playing the blame game, there are many strategies one can employ. Some are simple and straightforward, while others are more sophisticated and complex. Following is a brief description of some of the more common strategies:

1. *Denial.* Denial is the simplest blame game strategy. Denial is also unique in that it is the only strategy that does not require its users to blame anyone or anything else. To employ this tactic, all a person needs to do is say "I didn't do it" when an accusation is made, and "I don't know" when a question is asked. Although simple, the denial strategy can be very effective because regardless of what evidence is brought forward, all you have to do is continue playing dumb, and by playing dumb you'll avoid

saying anything that could incriminate yourself. The denial strategy is a favorite for those who have regular encounters with the law.

2. *Mysterious explanation.* The mysterious-explanation strategy is similar to the denial strategy in that the accused insist they are innocent. However, instead of playing dumb when evidence is brought forward, an accused person argues that there must be some mysterious explanation for what happened. This is the strategy employed by professional athletes when their drug tests come back positive and they argue that their blood must have somehow been tainted or that the lab must have made a mistake.

3. *Finger pointing.* The finger-pointing strategy is arguably the boldest strategy. In this approach a guilty party does not just claim to be innocent; a guilty party points to an innocent person and proclaims, "He did it!" To employ this strategy, you need to be a skilled liar, and you also need the conscience of a gnat.

4. *Blame the circumstances.* Blame the circumstances is the "I was in the wrong place at the wrong time" strategy. This is one of the weaker strategies because its success relies on receiving mercy. By blaming the circumstances, users argue that they would have done things differently if they could have, but the situation was out of their control, and therefore they did the best they could with the options they had. In today's hurried world, traffic has become a great circumstance to blame for being late to meetings and family gatherings. Some people even hope to get caught in a few minutes of traffic so they don't feel as though they're lying when they're an hour late.

5. *Blame an inanimate object.* Blame an inanimate object is the "sun got in my eyes" strategy. When people don't have a good explanation for a mistake they've made, they sometimes find an object to blame. The strength of this strategy lies in the inability of an inanimate object to defend itself. Take for example the fruit from the Tree of Knowledge of Good and Evil. For more than three thousand years people have been blaming the forbidden fruit for humankind's sinful nature, and as long as inanimate objects cannot defend their amoral character, people will continue to blame the forbidden fruit for their sins.

6. *Blame an animal.* Blame an animal is the "dog ate my homework" strategy. By blaming an animal, guilty parties admit some offense has occurred or a problem exists but claim it's not their fault. An animal in the road serves as a convenient defense for a car accident, squirrels and pesky rodents make wonderful excuses for unsolvable electrical problems, and of course how could I forget the old man who blames his dog for farting?

7. *Blame a spiritual being.* Blame a spiritual being is the "devil made me do it" strategy. This is a favorite tactic among religious people who look to blame the spiritual realm when things don't go their way. The Devil and his demons, however, are not the only spiritual beings blamed; some people blame God's failing to provide for their "needs" as justification for doing what seems right in their own eyes.

8. *Scapegoat.* The scapegoat strategy is the "throw your buddy under the bus" strategy. This is the strategy people use to shift blame away from themselves by identifying another guilty party as having been the mastermind behind the operation or for having forced or manipulated

them into being a party to the crime. Those who are obviously guilty and are trying to somehow mitigate their guilt or justify their involvement typically employ this strategy. This is the strategy I used to blame Danny for the fire-lighting fiasco I wrote about earlier.

9. *Justified.* The justified strategy is the lamest of all blame-game strategies. It's the approach guilty people take when they're caught red-handed and cannot think of any other strategy to employ. When guilty parties use this technique, they often try to make their offense the accuser's fault. For example, a woman confronts her husband with evidence that he's having an affair, and the husband responds by yelling, "How dare you invade my privacy! And, besides, if you hadn't let yourself go, this wouldn't have even happened!" This is a pitiful strategy; a person has to be a complete ass to use it.

10. *Victim.* The victim strategy is a sociopolitical strategy that allows people to argue they're victims of an "ism." Whether the claim is racism, sexism, classism, reverse discrimination-ism, or some other ism, the victim strategy allows its users to deny responsibility for their actions. Unfortunately, the liberal usage of this strategy for personal gain has desensitized many to the fact that discrimination is still a problem in society today.

11. *Blame an organization.* The blame-an-organization strategy is like the victim strategy in that it allows people to play the victim card. The difference, however, is that the blame-an-organization strategy points to a specific entity as the perpetrator that should be held responsible for the consequences of its "victims'" actions. Two prominent examples are tobacco companies being held responsible for causing cancer and fast food companies being blamed for America's obesity epidemic.

12. *Blame genetics.* The blame genetics strategy is a scientific strategy. Users of this tactic argue they are genetically predisposed to engage in certain deviant behaviors and therefore should not be held responsible for the actions caused by their genetic predisposition. Those with addiction issues and those who have difficulty controlling their impulses often use this strategy.

13. *Blame childhood.* The blame-childhood strategy is a complex psychological strategy. People who take this approach argue that the trauma and abuse they suffered in childhood have affected their personalities and that they should not be held responsible for the actions they perform or performed while under the influence of their disorders. Those who have anger-related problems and who commit acts of violence often use the blame-childhood strategy.

14. *Frame job.* The frame-job strategy is the most sinister of all blame-game strategies and the only one that requires a premeditated plan. When users of this strategy commit a crime, they plant evidence they hope will result in someone else being blamed for their crimes. A little brother who takes a few cookies from the cookie jar before dinner and plants crumbs in his sister's bedroom is using the frame-job strategy.

I could go on, and I'm sure you could add to the list, but I think fourteen strategies are sufficient to make the point: there are times we don't want to take responsibility for our own actions, and we play the blame game to avoid facing the truth.

When you think about it, a fascinating thing about the blame game is that nobody has to teach us how to play. Even a simple game of tic-tac-toe requires some explanation, but not the blame game. We all know how to play, and to be honest, it's second nature to us. In fact there are times when I don't even realize I'm being "that guy," trying to pass off blame for something I've obviously said or done.

I don't know what you felt while reading through the blame-game strategies, but in writing them I found myself laughing one moment and feeling ashamed the next. Some of the strategies are genuinely funny, but others are sad—very sad—as they expose the sad truth that in desperate moments we're willing to do or say anything to convince the world and ourselves we're not responsible for our own actions. This is one of those disturbing realizations we don't like to make, which is why we often don't even realize when we're playing the blame game. But in a world dying to control, we need to stop playing games and take responsibility for what we say and do.

Back in the garden of Eden, the conflict between man and God was reaching a climax. With Adam and Eve hiding from God among the trees, God called out to Adam, "Where are you?" inviting him to come out and confess to having eaten from the Tree of Knowledge of Good and Evil. Adam, however, didn't accept God's invitation. Instead of admitting what he'd done, Adam answered, "I heard you in the garden, and I was afraid because I was naked; so I hid." Realizing the bleak reality of the situation, Adam was too afraid and ashamed to confess that he'd eaten the forbidden fruit.

It was now God's turn to speak. Would God confront Adam with what he had done?

"And he said, 'Who told you that you were naked? Have you eaten from the tree that I commanded you not to eat from?'" Rather than confronting Adam with the facts, God responded by asking Adam more questions. Given the gravity of the situation and how this story is typically portrayed, you might think God would have directly addressed Adam, yelling something like, "Adam, stop hiding the truth! I know what you did. Now die and go to hell!" But that's not what God said. In fact, quite the opposite is true. God gave Adam a second chance. By asking more questions, God gave Adam another opportunity to admit to what he'd done. God didn't give up on Adam.

How about Adam? Had he given up on God?

"The man said, 'The woman you put here with me—she gave me some fruit from the tree, and I ate it.'" Again Adam refused to take responsibility for his actions. This time, instead of avoiding what he'd done, Adam played the blame game. "The woman—it's her fault!" Adam protested. No longer able to cover and hide the truth, Adam employed the scapegoat strategy, trying to shift all the blame onto Eve.

But was Adam blaming only Eve? In his response to God, Adam didn't simply say that the woman had given him fruit from the tree and that he'd eaten it. Adam said that the woman "you put here with me" had given him fruit from the tree and that he'd eaten it. Adam was pointing out the fact that God had placed Eve in the garden of Eden. But why? Why add the qualifier "you put here with me"? Why was Adam bringing God into it?

To understand the significance of Adam's statement, we need to look back to where Adam and Eve first entered the garden of Eden drama.

Adam and Eve were both introduced in Genesis 2. Genesis 2:7 reads, "The LORD formed the man from the dust of the ground and breathed into his nostrils the breath of life, and the man became a living being." Adam hadn't entered the drama by simply walking out onto the stage. God breathing Adam into existence was in itself a dramatic scene, portraying God as the Giver of life. Later, in verse 18, we read, "The LORD God said, 'It is not good for the man to be alone, I will make a helper suitable for him.'" This statement builds anticipation and sets the context for God's upcoming creation. In verses 21–22, Eve makes her entry.

²¹So the Lord God caused the man to fall into a deep sleep; and while he was sleeping, he took one of the man's ribs and closed up the place with flesh. ²²Then the Lord God made a woman from the rib he had taken out of the man, and he brought her to the man.

Eve's grand entrance into the drama speaks to God's intention of making a suitable helper for Adam. By fashioning Eve from one of Adam's ribs, God was displaying that Adam and Eve were of one flesh and that they were created to experience a partnership, an intimacy, with one another like no other beings in all God's creation. Then, to culminate his creative work, God presented Eve to Adam like a father proudly giving away his daughter in marriage.

With God responsible for creating a suitable helper for Adam, the intent of Adam's qualifier is clear. Adam was not just blaming Eve when he said, "The woman you put here with me—she gave me some fruit from the tree, and I ate it." Adam was blaming God. Adam might as well have said, "God, this is your fault—you were supposed to give me a suitable helper, but instead you made this defective woman who gave me some fruit from the tree, and I ate it." Unlike God, who didn't give up on his relationship with Adam, Adam appeared to have given up on his relationship with God.

How about Eve? Where did she stand with God?

"Then the Lord God said to the woman, 'What is this you have done?'" As he had done with Adam, God asked Eve a question, giving her an opportunity to confess to eating the forbidden fruit. How did Eve respond to God?

"The woman said, 'The serpent deceived me, and I ate.'" Like Adam, Eve refused to take responsibility for her actions. She too played the blame game, using the "devil made me do it" strategy. Like her partner Adam, Eve was more concerned with trying to preserve self than with restoring her severed relationship with God.

After eating from the Tree of Knowledge of Good and Evil, Adam and Eve wanted nothing to do with God. When they heard God walking in the garden of Eden, they hid from him among the trees. When God called out to Adam, "Where are you?" Adam offered a lame excuse for hiding. When God asked Adam what had happened, Adam blamed Eve for giving him the forbidden fruit, and he blamed God for giving him an inadequate helper. Finally, when God asked Eve what she had done, Eve blamed the serpent. After eating the forbidden fruit, Adam and Eve did all they could to avoid God, and when God brought the truth to light, Adam and Eve refused to take responsibility for violating their personal relationship with God.

Yet despite all that Adam and Eve had done—the betraying, the covering, the hiding, and the blaming—God didn't give up on his relationship with humankind. God pursued Adam and Eve again and again.

What overwhelms me most about God's pursuit of Adam and Eve is not his undying commitment to humankind; what overwhelms me most is how God's reaching out to Adam and Eve seems to contradict a fundamental tenet of the Judeo-Christian belief system. Central to both Judaism and Christianity is the doctrine that sin and sinful beings cannot exist in the holy presence of God, but in the garden of Eden drama—the story that explains when and how sin entered the human race—God is portrayed as one who reaches out to sinful humanity.

It appears that what we have here is yet another blame-game strategy. To say that sin and sinful beings cannot exist in the holy presence of God is to *blame sin* for the distance we experience in our relationship with God. The problem, though, is not that sin cannot exist in the presence of God; the problem in the God-human personal relationship is that sinful beings don't want to be in the presence of God; sinful beings would rather *be* God.

In summary, humans want to be like God, knowing good and evil. We want to be in control, doing what seems right in our own eyes, eating more and more forbidden fruit as we try to enjoy the ride on the merryless-go-round. To perpetuate the illusion of being in control and the delusion that we can sustain our own existence, we live like mannequins on display, covering and hiding the naked truth of who we are, what we think, and the shameful things we've said and done. Furthermore, if some truth comes to light, a truth that leads us to feel naked and ashamed, all we have to do is play the blame game to regain the illusion of being in control and to feel justified in having done what seemed right in our own eyes. This is the endless cycle that comes with eating from the Tree of Knowledge of Good and Evil. This is the story of dying to control.

PART II

THE KNOWLEDGE OF GOOD AND EVIL

CHAPTER 5

~

THE WORLD ACCORDING TO ME

"**W**HY CAN'T WE just get along?" Have you ever asked yourself that question? Or have you ever stepped back, looked at the world, and wondered why everybody seems to be fighting? It's crazy—all fighting is crazy—and I don't just mean the wars, political conflict, civil unrest, and terrorist attacks that happen around us; I'm also referring to the fights we personally find ourselves in—the jockeying for position in rush-hour traffic; the maneuvering and backstabbing at work; the dealing with children who refuse to eat their vegetables; and the spousal disagreements, family disputes, and countless other squabbles we find ourselves in every day. These personal fights keep us awake at night; we lose sleep wondering, "Why can't we just get along?"

Our struggle to get along is not a new phenomenon; it's at least as old as recorded history. Whether written on tablets, tombs, pyramids, or papyri, accounts of ancient civilizations are full of strife, betrayal, and war. In fact, as far as I know, we've yet to discover a utopian society void of horrific conflict. Why is that? What is it about human nature that keeps us from getting along?

The garden of Eden drama—the story of a perfect world gone wrong—offers an answer. However, for much of the last century our society has been more interested in fighting over whether the account is historical than in discussing this historic account of why we fight. As a result, when it comes to knowing about what happened in the garden of Eden, people tend to be more familiar with the flannelgraph version they learned during childhood than with the actual biblical account and therefore are generally unaware of the story's insights into human nature.

One critical difference between the children's story of Adam and Eve and the biblical account is the central point of conflict. In the Bible the conflict centers around the knowledge of good and evil, but in the children's story the conflict centers around the forbidden fruit. It is understandable that the children's story would focus on a concrete object—fruit—as opposed to an abstract concept—the knowledge of good and evil, but it's important to note that the difference significantly affects the story.

When the forbidden fruit is portrayed as the central point of conflict, the storyline revolves around the fruit—how Adam and Eve were not supposed to eat the fruit, how they ate the fruit, and how they were punished for having eaten the fruit. Told in this fashion, the story is a simplistic lesson on the importance of obedience, how acts of disobedience are acts of sin, and how sin has consequences—sometimes serious and deadly consequences. Although all these points may be true, they don't accurately reflect the main storyline in the garden of Eden drama.

In contrast, when the knowledge of good and evil is portrayed as the central point of conflict, the story line revolves around the knowledge of good and evil—how Adam and Eve acquired the knowledge of good and evil, how they changed after they acquired the knowledge of good and evil, and how God responded to their having acquired the knowledge of good and evil. Told in this fashion, the story is a complex commentary on human nature and interpersonal relationships.

In short, rather than being a children's story about forbidden fruit, the account of Adam and Eve is a sophisticated drama about the knowledge of good and evil. Hence, God began His closing monologue by saying, "The man has now become like one of us, knowing good and evil. ..." God didn't begin the monologue by saying, "Now that man has eaten the forbidden fruit..." God didn't focus on the forbidden fruit, because the story is not about the fruit; it's about humankind becoming like God, knowing good and evil.

Once you start reading the garden of Eden drama without the fairy-tale bias of magical fruit, the story comes alive, and your eyes open to several questions: What is the knowledge of good and evil? Why didn't God want humankind to have it? In what capacity did Adam and Eve become like God? These are the questions the story begs its audience to ask, but they're questions that in the end the story only vaguely answers, leaving the audience to contemplate the meaning of the knowledge of good and evil and what it means for humankind to have it.

It is here, in fleshing out this forbidden knowledge, that we'll find our answer to the question, "Why can't we just get along?"

⁓

Although the knowledge of good and evil is not widely discussed today, it's a subject that some of the most influential theologians in Christian history have addressed. Irenaeus (c. 130–200) and Tertullian (c. 155–220) wrote about humankind acquiring the knowledge of good and evil in the second century, when Christianity was just beginning to establish some of its core doctrines. Augustine (354–430), often called the Father of the Western Church because of his significant role in shaping Western theology, offered two interpretations on the subject of humankind becoming like God, knowing good and evil. And more recently, during the Protestant Reformation, Martin Luther (1483–1546) and John Calvin

(1509–64) had some strong words regarding humankind's attempt to acquire the knowledge of good and evil. All these important figures argued for their beliefs during times of doctrinal dispute, and, interestingly, their interpretations of humankind acquiring the knowledge of good and evil figured in the disputes they were facing. The following historical survey briefly describes each theologian's context for writing and each one's interpretations of humankind acquiring the knowledge of good and evil, particularly as it relates to God's statement that "The man has now become like one of us, knowing good and evil."

Historical Survey

Irenaeus

In the second century, when Christianity was gaining popularity, there was another emerging religious movement known as Gnosticism. Irenaeus was concerned with how Gnostic teachings were influencing the Christian faith and he harshly criticized Gnostic doctrines, going as far as saying that Gnosticism was not Christian heresy but a false religion.[5]

Gnostics and Christians had very different ideas about creation, Adam and Eve, and the knowledge of good and evil. Gnostics believed that the physical world was an evil creation of the *demiurge*—a lesser power beneath the Supreme God—and that in this evil world some human beings had trapped within them a divine spark that could be freed from the human body and return to the spiritual realm. It was further believed that freedom came through the acquisition of *gnosis*, the knowledge of the truth that the physical world was evil and that the creator god of the Old Testament was actually the demiurge and not the Supreme God.[6]

As for the knowledge of good and evil, Gnosticism taught that the demiurge attempted to keep Adam and Eve ignorant of the truth by not allowing them to eat from the Tree of Knowledge of Good and Evil. Thus, Gnostics believed that once Adam and Eve ate the forbidden fruit they were enlightened to the truth, and the divine spark within them was free to return to the spiritual realm.[7]

In arguing against Gnosticism, Irenaeus taught that death, not freedom, came upon Adam and Eve when they ate the forbidden fruit in disobedience to the one true God.[8] As for their acquiring the knowledge of good and evil, Irenaeus wrote that when Adam and Eve ate the fruit, they lost their "natural disposition and child-like mind, and had come to the knowledge of evil things."[9]

Tertullian

A second-century contemporary of Irenaeus, Tertullian was also concerned about the influence that the Gnostic doctrines, as well as the teachings of Marcion[10] (d. ca. 160), could have on the Christian faith. In particular, Tertullian sought to refute the belief that the entire physical world, including the human body, was evil, and that the creator God of the Old Testament was a lesser God than the God of the New Testament. It was in this context that Tertullian offered a unique interpretation of God's statement that "the man has now become like one of us, knowing good and evil." Tertullian believed God's statement was a prophetic proclamation that humankind would someday in the future be like God, sharing in God's eternal glory through the saving work of Jesus Christ.[11] This interpretation allowed Tertullian to maintain continuity between the God of the Old Testament and the God of the New Testament. This interpretation also allowed Tertullian to argue for the goodness of the human body, writing that every person's flesh will rise again "in its own identity, in its own integrity" through Jesus Christ as Mediator, "who shall reconcile both God to man, and man to God; the spirit to the flesh, and the flesh to the spirit."[12]

Augustine

Augustine, writing in the late fourth century and early fifth century, directed his early work against Manicheanism—a religion with many similarities to Gnosticism. In interpreting Genesis 3:22, Augustine held that God's statement was intended as a figure of speech that could be taken in one of two ways. First, it could be understood as God mocking humankind for thinking we could be like God by eating from the Tree of Knowledge of Good and Evil.[13] This interpretation refuted the notion that Adam and Eve were somehow enlightened when they ate the forbidden fruit.

Augustine's second interpretation was consistent with Irenaeus's response to Gnosticism. Augustine argued that if Adam and Eve had obeyed God, they would have experienced only that which was good, but because of their disobedience they would experience the evil that had previously existed only in the mind of God. Adam and Eve had become like God in that God's knowledge of good and evil would now be experienced by all humanity.[14]

Martin Luther

Martin Luther, a key figure in the Protestant Reformation, had numerous doctrinal disputes with the Roman Catholic Church, but none as significant as the fight over the means to salvation. In contrast to Roman Catholic tradition, Luther believed that human beings were totally depraved, so therefore salvation was achieved by faith alone and not by a comingling of faith and good works. Living at a time when there was a growing optimism in the potential of humankind, Luther dedicated much of his writing to describing humanity's utter wickedness and complete dependence upon God's grace for salvation. In his commentary on Genesis, Luther argued that God's statement that people had become like God, knowing good and evil, were words of "bitter sarcasm."[15] He further argued that even though humanity had already lost its glory and fallen into sin and death, God spoke these words as additional rebuke for two clear reasons:

> God saw how badly Adam's descendants would turn out. Therefore He gave him this message which he was to tell his children, namely, that man had become like the Devil in trying to become like God, contrary to His Word. This was to warn them not to add to the sin of their parents and increase their own transgression by departing from God ever more and more. God [also] wanted man to long for the image of God, which he had lost, and to oppose sin all the more as the cause of his misery.[16]

John Calvin

John Calvin, another key figure in the Protestant Reformation, interpreted God's statement in Genesis 3:22 in much the same way as Luther. With respect to God saying, "The man has now become like one of us," Calvin wrote, "An ironical reproof, by which God would not only prick the heart of man, but pierce it through and through."[17] And as for humankind "knowing good and evil," Calvin wrote,

> "To know good and evil," describes the cause of so great misery, namely, that Adam, not content with his condition, had tried to ascend higher than was lawful ... Thus was it necessary, for his iron pride to be beaten down, that he might at length descend into himself, and become more and more displeased with himself.[18]

Contemporary Survey

Once we reached the twentieth century, interpretations of the knowledge of good and evil focused more on supporting or condemning cultural realities than on engaging doctrinal disputes. The purpose of the following survey is to highlight four common interpretations of the knowledge of good and evil espoused in America during the twentieth century. (For those interested in learning more about the four positions, see endnotes 19, 22, 25 and 26 for a list of sources for each position.)

Universal Knowledge

Noting the intellectual and technological advancements of humankind in the twentieth century, we begin this contemporary survey with the interpretation of universal knowledge.[19] According to Von Rad,

> Knowledge of good and evil means, therefore, omniscience in the widest sense of the word … Man has stepped outside the state of dependence, he has refused obedience and willed to make himself independent. The guiding principle of his life is no longer obedience but his autonomous knowing and willing, and thus he has really ceased to understand himself as creature.[20]

In this light the universal knowledge position holds that humankind has left a childlike state, no longer dependent upon a father, and has become like God in that each person is independent to learn of the outside world.[21] Thus there is no longer any limit to the breadth of humankind's knowledge.

Sexual Knowledge

In the twentieth century, sex has seemingly found its way into every conversation, and the knowledge of good and evil is no exception.[22] The sexual knowledge interpretation suggests that in eating the forbidden fruit, humankind either became aware of the physical difference between the male and female anatomy, or humankind became like God in gaining the ability to beget life. Reicke argued, "The fruit of the prohibited tree opens their eyes to sex: that must not be forgotten. Accordingly 'good and evil,' while properly referring to 'everything,' is here used as a euphemism for the secret of sex."[23] In terms of humankind being able to produce life, Engnell wrote, "The expression undoubtedly refers to the sexual sphere. Adam is now like the 'gods' in that respect too, that he is now capable of begetting. The whole stress is laid on the ability to procreate."[24]

Ethical and Moral Discrimination

After the sexual-knowledge interpretation, it seems fitting to present the interpretation of ethical and moral discrimination.[25] Unlike most other positions, this interpretation is held by a wide range of theologians, from the most liberal to the most conservative, who believe that in eating the forbidden fruit humankind acquired a conscience—the capacity to discriminate between good and evil. Proponents of this interpretation further believe that humankind was ultimately supposed to gain this knowledge, but there's a lack of agreement over the "goodness" of the way this knowledge was acquired. Some believe that it was right for Adam and Eve to have eaten the forbidden fruit, while others believe Adam and Eve prematurely gained this knowledge by disobeying God, and still others hold different nuanced positions as to how humankind was supposed to gain the capacity for ethical and moral discrimination.

Understanding Inner Dynamics

An interpretation of the knowledge of good and evil that has gained recent support is that of humankind acquiring the ability to understand the inner dynamics of the workings of the cosmos.[26] In support of this position, Stern wrote,

> The phrase seems to mean the following: When Adam ate the fruit he acquired a knowledge of evil which may have included unnatural sexual acts. However, it was also a knowledge which made him godlike, so it must have been a wisdom which included the secret processes of things. These included various magical arts and possibly certain technical arts. This now gave man a wide range of possibilities from which he could choose. He was no longer bound to his instinctual desires and the ground was laid for committing evil.[27]

In other words, Adam's "field of operations in which he could exercise his powers was greatly widened. He could now perform evil acts of which he had no knowledge before."[28]

In looking over the numerous interpretations of God's statement that "The man has now become like one of us, knowing good and evil," I think it is fair to say that Augustine was correct when he wrote that this is an "ambiguous expression."[29] Without a historical or contemporary consensus, we're left to answer for ourselves the questions the story begs the audience to ask: What is the knowledge of good and evil? Why did God not want humankind to have it? In what capacity did Adam and Eve become like God?

In the remainder of this chapter I offer answers to these questions that I believe honor many past interpretations while recognizing the realities of life in the twenty-first century.

A common theme across many of the interpretations is the idea that upon eating the forbidden fruit, Adam and Eve left a childlike state of dependence upon God and ventured out on their own to explore the world. Irenaeus wrote that Adam and Eve left their "natural disposition and child-like mind, and had come to the knowledge of evil things."[30] Augustine wrote that humankind would now experience the evil that once existed only in the mind of God. Von Rad wrote: "Man has stepped outside the state of dependence, he has refused obedience and willed to make himself independent."[31] And Stern wrote that man "was no longer bound to his instinctual desires and the ground was laid for committing evil."[32] What these and other interpretations have in common is the notion that by eating the forbidden fruit, Adam and Eve declared their independence from God. From there, each interpretation goes on to explain the knowledge of good and evil in the context of a doctrinal dispute or to explain a cultural reality. But what if the knowledge of good and evil in its broadest sense is simply human beings declaring their independence from God, making self the arbiter of good and evil?

The arbiter of good and evil interpretation seems to be the position that Thomas Aquinas (1225–74) had in mind in the thirteenth century and Dietrich Bonhoeffer (1906–45) espoused in the 1930s. In his *Summa Theologica*, Aquinas wrote, "But the first man sinned chiefly by coveting God's likeness ... namely that by his own natural power he might decide what was good and what was evil for him to do."[33] In the same vein, Bonhoeffer wrote,

> There can at this point be no more doubt that the serpent was right in the promise it made. The Creator confirms the truth of that promise: Humankind has become like one of us. It is *sicut*

deus [like God]. Humankind has got what it wants; it has itself become creator, source of life, fountainhead of the knowledge of good and evil. It is alone by itself, it lives out of its own resources, it no longer needs any others, it is the lord of its own world, even though that does mean now that it is the solitary lord and despot of its own mute, violated, silenced, dead, ego-world.[34]

By becoming their own arbiters of good and evil, Adam and Eve had essentially become their own gods. This is a bold interpretation of the knowledge of good and evil, but I believe it's an appropriate one for our day. For much of the modern era humankind has maintained a profound optimism for what it could and would accomplish. Our ability to figure out the inner workings of matter, observe the outer reaches of the universe, and devise extravagant theories has allowed us to conceive of life without God. The more knowledge we gain, the more technology we develop, and the more we're able to sustain our own existence, the less we see our need for God or even the thought of God. In the twenty-first century, to eat from the Tree of Knowledge of Good and Evil is to become your own god, viewing self as the arbiter of good and evil.

To explain what it looks like for humankind to have acquired the knowledge of good and evil, let's begin with a diagram that shows what life would have been like before Adam and Eve ate from the Tree of Knowledge of Good and Evil.

God's Knowledge

Good	Evil

I refer to this diagram as God's T (pronounced *tee*). Before Adam and Eve ate the forbidden fruit, life was straightforward. Whatever God declared as good was good and whatever God declared as evil was evil. There was no confusion, no debate. Everything was either good or evil based on God's T.

The moment Adam and Eve ate the fruit from the Tree of Knowledge of Good and Evil, they rejected God's T. What God had declared as being evil—eating the forbidden fruit—Adam and Eve declared as being good. Adam and Eve rejected God's authority; they rejected God's T. In eating the fruit from the Tree of Knowledge of Good and Evil, Adam and Eve became their own arbiters of good and evil, and they began seeing the world from their own Ts.

Adam's Knowledge

Good	Evil

Eve's Knowledge

Good	Evil

If you'll notice, in becoming their own arbiters of good and evil, Adam and Eve each established their own distinct Ts. Because they both chose to eat the forbidden fruit, they both declared their independence from God, and therefore by their own free will Adam and Eve each became their own arbiters of good and evil.

The all-important question then is, how do Adam's T and Eve's T align with God's T? Assuming that God is still the ultimate Arbiter of good and evil, how do Adam and Eve's Ts fit with God's T?

To use Adam as the example, where would you place Adam's T on a diagram of God's T? Would Adam's T overlap in some fashion with God's T? Would some of Adam's Good be God's Good, and some of Adam's Evil be God's Evil? Take a minute to think about it. Where would you place Adam's T?

God's Knowledge

Good		Evil

Based on my experience with teaching Genesis 3, most people place Adam's T on a diagram of God's T as follows:

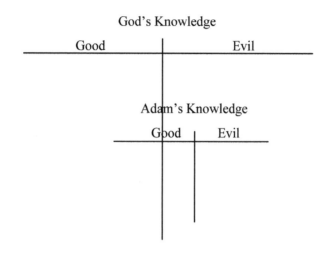

Viewed this way, Adam's having acquired the knowledge of good and evil means that Adam gained an understanding of God's Good but gained only a partial understanding of God's Evil. With some of the Good in Adam's T crossing into the Evil of God's T, there are things that Adam thought were Good that God called Evil—things such as eating the forbidden fruit—things that religious people call sin.

However, as I see it, to overlap Adam's T with God's T is to misunderstand the fundamental problem of humankind acquiring the knowledge of good and evil. Instead of overlapping Adam's T with God's T, I would place all Adam's T on the evil side of God's T, as follows:

God's Knowledge

Good | Evil

Adam's Knowledge

Good | Evil

Adam's T belongs on the evil side of God's T because from God's perspective, for Adam to function as the arbiter of good and evil would be inherently evil; Adam would be undermining God and usurping God's authority by viewing himself as the ultimate judge of good and evil. For humankind to exalt self in this manner is what some people refer to as humankind's sinful nature, or the depravity of man; it's the idea that we can reject God's authority and live as we please, each deciding for ourselves what is good and what is evil.

To see oneself as the arbiter of good and evil has some troubling implications. Bonhoeffer put it this way:

> For what causes despair in Adam's situation is just this, that Adam lives out of Adam's own resources, is imprisoned within Adam, and thus can want only Adam, can hanker only after Adam; for Adam had indeed become Adam's own god, the creator of Adam's own life. When Adam seeks God, when Adam seeks life, Adam seeks only Adam.[35]

As soon as Adam ate from the Tree of Knowledge of Good and Evil, Adam's world began to revolve around Adam. Self-absorbed, the first thing Adam saw was his own nakedness. He then covered himself and hid from God to preserve the illusion that he was in control. And because Adam viewed himself as the arbiter of good and evil, when God confronted him with the truth of what he had done, Adam wouldn't admit he was wrong. Why should he have? Adam had become his own god. He couldn't have been wrong—how can a god be wrong? That's why Adam blamed Eve for giving him the forbidden fruit and why he had the audacity to blame God for giving him that "defective" woman. Adam was preserving his position as the arbiter of good and evil, he was preserving his T, he was preserving the delusion that he could be his own god.

Bonhoeffer's commentary on humankind's acquisition of the knowledge of good and evil and Adam's self-absorption was not just theological abstraction. Bonhoeffer had the unfortunate opportunity to witness unbridled humanity functioning at its worst. It was during his winter semester in 1932–33 at the University of Berlin that the Third Reich originated and Bonhoeffer wrote his commentary on the story of Adam and Eve. As the years went on, Bonhoeffer saw Adolf Hitler's T in its perverse glory as the self-absorbed madman tried to establish himself as the arbiter of good and evil for the entire world.

Tragically, due to his opposition of Hitler and Nazism, Bonhoeffer was arrested in April 1943 and executed in April 1945.

This is not what God intended. God did not want humankind to have the knowledge of good and evil. It's too much for us to handle. The enormity of it swallows us, and not just people like Hitler who rise to positions of great power; the knowledge of good and evil gets the best of all of us. All of us in our own ways live in our own Ts, in a world according to *me*. We all want what we want when we want it. We all want to do what seems right in our own eyes. We all ride the merryless-go-round, and when life stops working, we live like mannequins on display, protecting and preserving the illusion that we're in control and the delusion that we can be our own gods. Even when our delusional world starts falling apart, we can play the blame game forever, never having to admit when we're wrong, each of us preserving our own T.

This is why we fight. This is why we can't get along. Our Ts clash. We each think "I know what's best!" "I deserve to go next!" "Nobody has the right to tell me what to do!" We each try to live in a world according to me—each of us trying to live according to our own Ts.

This is the world dying to control, a world described in the first four chapters, but we don't have to keep living this way. There's another option. In the remaining four chapters we will examine our twenty-first-century dilemma of dying to control with the hope we can change.

PART III

THE 21ST CENTURY DILEMMA

Chapter 6

Curses! Curses? Curses

[14]So the LORD God said to the serpent,
"Because you have done this,
Cursed are you above all the livestock
and all the wild animals!
You will crawl on your belly
and you will eat dust
all the days of your life.

[15]And I will put enmity
between you and the woman,
and between your offspring and hers;
he will crush your head,
and you will strike his heel."

[16]To the woman he said,
"I will greatly increase your pains in childbearing;
with pain you will give birth to children.
Your desire will be for your husband,
and he will rule over you."

^{17}To Adam he said, "Because you listened to
your wife and ate from the tree about which I
commanded you, 'You must not eat of it,'
Cursed is the ground because of you;
through painful toil you will eat of it
all the days of your life.

^{18}It will produce thorns and thistles for you,
and you will eat the plants of the field.

^{19}By the sweat of your brow
you will eat your food
until you return to the ground,
since from it you were taken;
for dust you are
and to dust you will return."

—Genesis 3:14–19

T HE TIME HAD come for God to take control of the situation.
Because Adam and Eve were playing the blame game instead
of taking responsibility for their actions, God asserted his authority.
Often referred to as "the curse" or "the curse of man," God proclaimed
judgment upon each participant in the garden of Eden who played a
role in Adam and Eve eating the fruit from the Tree of Knowledge of
Good and Evil. God said to the serpent, "Cursed are you above all the
livestock and all the wild animals! You will crawl on your belly and
you will eat dust all the days of your life." To Eve he said, "I will greatly
increase your pains in childbearing; with pain you will give birth to
children." And to Adam he said, "Cursed is the ground because of you;
through painful toil you will eat of it all the days of your life."

This judgment that fell upon Adam and Eve has impacted all
humanity. Whether we're the literal or figurative descendants of
Adam and Eve, we all feel the weight of the curse. Every civilization
has to struggle with the threats of wild animals, the complications of

childbearing, and the stubborn earth not wanting to produce food or at least produce it easily. With life on earth being so hard, as the Judeo-Christian faith spread around the world, so did the account of "the curse of man" and the fear that God punishes all who disobey his law. This fear of punishment can be found in Judeo-Christian cultures all around the world.

Take my story for example. Although I was born and raised in the United States, my family is of Ukrainian descent, and I grew up in a Ukrainian home. We spoke Ukrainian, we ate Ukrainian food, we honored Ukrainian customs, we attended a Ukrainian Catholic church, and I even went to Ukrainian school on Saturday mornings until my parents finally stopped making me go. Don't get me wrong; I'm proud of my heritage, but I just didn't want to go to school on Saturday mornings. Can you blame me?

Anyway, to my point, Ukrainian, as do all languages, has many expressions that communicate the values and beliefs of its people. One such expression best translates into English as "God punished you." In the Ukrainian community I was a part of, it was believed that God would punish you when you sin. Therefore I was raised to believe that every time I sinned, God was watching, looming, prepared to punish me in some fashion.

Not only did we believe that God punished us for our sins, but we also made the point of using the expression at opportune moments with one another. So for example if I was sent to my room for teasing my older sister and along the way I stubbed my toe, someone would say, "See? God punished you!" Over time it got to the point that whenever something went wrong I'd wonder if God was punishing me for my sin.

Today I see the world differently, but those words "God punished you" still echo in my mind, and every so often, when something goes awry, I wonder what I might have done wrong.

My story is unfortunately not unique. If you were raised in an ethnic community steeped in Christian tradition, or a strict Catholic family, or a fundamentalist/evangelical home, you may be able to relate to my story. You may know this fear of punishment, believing that God is waiting to cast judgment upon you for some sin you've committed.

This teaching that God cursed humankind in the garden of Eden and that God is prepared to punish you too may help churches manage their congregants and parents control their children, but is it an accurate reflection of God in the garden of Eden? Sure, the Bible speaks about the wrath of God and God's judgment, but did God curse Adam and Eve after they ate the forbidden fruit?

If you look at the entire garden of Eden drama, the word "curse" is used only twice—in verses 3:14 and 3:17. In verse 3:14 God said to the serpent, "Cursed are you above all the livestock and all the wild animals! You will crawl on your belly and you will eat dust all the days of your life." By cursing the serpent "above" the livestock and wild animals, God was cursing all the animals, but he was cursing the serpent more than the others. (In Middle Eastern culture the ground is seen as dirty and unclean, so to make the serpent "crawl on [its] belly" and "eat dust" was to treat the serpent more harshly than other animals.)

Then, in verse 17, God said to Adam, "Cursed is the ground because of you; through painful toil you will eat of it all the days of your life." If you'll notice, God cursed the ground, not Adam. If God's intention was to curse man, he could have said, "I curse you, Adam, by making the ground hard to cultivate." Yet that isn't what God said.

In verses 3:14 and 3:17 God cursed the animals and the ground; God never cursed humankind. Yes, God gave the woman "pain" in childbirth (the subject of the next chapter), but it is not called a curse. We need to be careful not to infer that God cursed the woman because God never cursed the man. The curses in Genesis 3 are not the curse of man, the curse of woman, or the curse of humankind. God didn't curse human beings; he cursed the animals and the ground, and this distinction makes all the difference.

To curse someone is to wish that person misfortune or doom. Curses tend to be spiteful or vindictive, and they typically don't have redemptive intentions. To say that God cursed humankind in Genesis 3 is to portray God as a bit of a tyrant who has no tolerance for sin or sinful people. Please do not hear me trying to soften the character of God. God, as sovereign Ruler, has the prerogative to do as he pleases, and the Bible contains plenty of stories of God exercising his wrath against sin. I'm not questioning God's disdain for sin; I'm questioning the teaching of "the curse."

In the first chapter of Genesis we are told:

> 27So God created man in his own image, in the image of God he created him; male and female he created them.
>
> 28God blessed them and said to them, "Be fruitful and increase in number; fill the earth and subdue it. Rule over the fish of the sea and the birds of the air and over every living creature that moves on the ground."
>
> 29Then God said, "I give you every seed-bearing plant on the face of the whole earth and every tree that has fruit with seed in it. They will be yours for food.

In the beginning, human beings were created in the image of God and given the privilege and responsibility of ruling over the earth. Yet because we ate the forbidden fruit—doing what seemed right in our own eyes—we lost perspective. We each began living in our own T, thinking we could decide for ourselves what is good and evil. We began to think having control over the earth was our right rather than a privilege given to us by God.

So what God did was curse the two realms he'd given us to rule—the animals and the ground. In instituting the curse, God was helping us to regain perspective. Having to fight off wild animals and struggle with the ground for food humbles us and helps us to see ourselves for what we really are. When God ends the curse by telling Adam, "for dust you are and to dust you will return," God is reminding us of what has always been true—that he is the Creator and that we are the created, and that apart from him there is no life.

So how then should we view the curses in Genesis 3?

I am convinced that the curses are not the curse of man but God's provision for humankind. I believe that through the curses God is seeking to restore his trust relationship with every human being. We can see God's commitment to us in his final words to the serpent: "he will crush your head, and you will strike his heel." These words speak to something more than just the conflict that man will have with animals. These words are an allusion to Jesus and his conflict with the Devil. In the curses God is foreshadowing his redemptive plan for humankind.

Instead of viewing the curses as God damning us, we should see them as God pursuing us. Instead of blaming God for the curse, we should see the curses as an opportunity to trust God as the Sustainer of life.

Can you imagine what a perfect world would look like if we didn't have to struggle with animals and the ground and we could all walk around with the delusion that we were gods, each of us actually entitled to live according to our own T? You think it's hard for us to get along now? By cursing the animals and the ground, God was making it clear he alone is the Arbiter of good and evil and the Sustainer of life. God instituted the curses to draw us back to himself so that we might find life in him.

~

The illusion of control vanished as people across Washington, DC, Virginia, and Maryland feared for their lives. There was at least one sniper on the loose, randomly shooting individuals in shopping center parking lots and gas stations. As panic settled over the Washington metropolitan area, people began to look over their shoulders as they loaded groceries and pumped gas into their cars, hoping, praying, that they would not be next.

After three weeks of terror, on October 24, 2002, two perpetrators were apprehended at a rest stop off an interstate highway. The ordeal had finally come to an end but tragically not before ten people had been killed and three others seriously wounded by the Beltway snipers.

Horrific stories like this one are disturbing. Somewhere deep within our beings, maybe in our souls, we feel a most unsettling angst—one that tends to linger. Death can have this effect on us, particularly in situations where it could have been avoided, or in this case when it is a random, senseless act of violence. It just feels wrong.

Beyond the tragic loss of life, there's something else about an event like this that disturbs us—the jarring realization that we're not in control of our lives as much as we'd like to think. The idea that I could be shot while loading groceries into my car reminds me that I do not sustain my own life. Sure, we can avoid dangerous situations and take meticulous care of our bodies, but ultimately we're not in control. There are countless internal and external variables that could end our lives in an instant. A blood vessel could burst in my brain as I type these words and there would be nothing I could do about it; a drunk driver could hit me head-on before I have a second to react; a tidal wave could wash over my family as we stand helplessly on the beach; and a giant asteroid could be hurling toward Earth, and the only thing we could do would be to count down the seconds until impact. We are at the mercy of the world around us, and we need our bodies to perform countless involuntary functions to keep us alive. That's part of why hearing a story about madmen randomly shooting people is so troublesome; it's a shocking reminder that life is fragile and that we do not have ultimate control over our lives. Death, without warning, can visit any one of us at any time.

However, in twenty-first-century America, we live with the illusion that we're in control of our lives. Most mornings when we get out of bed, we expect to return to our pillows that evening. The average American has no reason to think otherwise, and so understandably we assume each day we'll live for yet another day.

We're able to live with this illusion of control because technology has helped us mitigate the curses. Most Americans don't have to fight off wild animals. Thanks to gunpowder, pesticides, vaccines, and other modern developments, we've regained control over much of the animal world. As for our struggle with the ground, irrigation techniques, genetic engineering of plants, modern machinery, and advancements in weather forecasting and seismology have helped us manage and even at times control our groaning planet. We've mitigated the curses to a greater degree than any other people in human history, and as technology continues to progress, so will our illusion of control.

The fact remains, though, that the curses are still a conscious reality for most people in the world today. The possibility of being bitten by a deadly snake is a legitimate fear for more than a billion people in our world, and acquiring food and clean water is a daily struggle for the majority of the earth's population. With so many people living on the brink of death, it is staggering to think that the closest we as average Americans will get to realizing the daily struggle for food and water is the fear of being shot by a sniper as we load groceries into our cars.

I'm not suggesting we should feel guilty for our good fortune or stop utilizing modern technology. What I'm saying is that our good fortune has led to a loss of perspective. Technology feeds the illusion of control so much so that it is easy for us to think that we don't need God, that we can sustain ourselves, and that we can tame our groaning planet. As a result, we're consumed with self-preservation. Instead of focusing on today, we worry about tomorrow. Instead of being content with what we have, we search for what we think we need.

As we pursue self-preservation, life is passing us by. We want to believe that "there's always tomorrow," which is why death, particularly the unexpected death of a loved one, leaves us questioning how we spend our time today. In mitigating the curses, we seem to be losing sight of what really matters—life together.

If you look at past civilizations and societies around the world today, at the center of life and culture you'll find the communal meal. As we scarf down our fast food, rushing from one place to another, trying to sustain our own existence, most of the world takes time to be together and appreciate what they have. When you think about it, is there anything more central to life than sitting around a table of food and drink with the people you love? The curses were intended to give us perspective. The curses were intended to help us see what really matters—enjoying life together in the midst of the bounty of food and drink God has provided.

As technology continues to advance in the twenty-first century, offering us more and more control over the curses, who or what will we trust to sustain our lives? Will we spend more time pursuing the illusion of control? Will we commit more energy to preserving our own existence? Will we become more adept at playing the blame game? Or will we become more grateful for what we have, take more responsibility for our actions, and regain perspective on what really matters in life?

To use my favorite mixed metaphor, "this is where the rubber meets the chicken." After years of studying and preparing, the time had come for me to cross the road and hope for the best; it was time to put my vision into practice.

A few months earlier my wife and I had flown to central New York to meet with a group of people starting a new church. They brought us in to evaluate whether I was the right person to pastor their congregation, and we were there to discern whether this was the place we were called to do ministry. One evening we met with a group of about thirty people in the host's living room. Sitting in a circle of couches and folding chairs, we were engaged in small talk when I threw myself out there, saying something like, "Okay, I'm sure you all have a lot of questions for me, so go ahead and ask me whatever you want."

For the next two to three hours I answered their questions and laid out my vision for "creating a safe environment for experiencing God-centered life change." I explained my thoughts on the garden of Eden drama and how I believed that most Christians don't live in the freedom they claim to possess. As I often do, I got passionate as I spoke about how God is calling out to all of us, "Where are you?", but like Adam and Eve we hide in darkness from God and from one another.

As they continued asking questions about this vision, I talked about how we cover and hide the truth of who we are, what we think, and the shameful deeds we have done, and how our covering and hiding results in us missing out on the fullness of life that God created us to experience.

As the evening progressed, people in the room caught the vision, and we began to explore the possibilities of what a church like this could bring to central New York. The idea of creating a safe place for people to come out of hiding, deal with their personal problems and issues, and experience life together was exciting. Everyone seemed to agree with and share our enthusiasm. Later that night, Anne-Marie and I had a hard time falling asleep as we were convinced this was the place we needed to be. We returned home with the hope that they would offer me the position, and a few weeks later they did.

In August 2001 we crossed the road and stepped into Utica, New York. When we arrived, there were fifty or so people committed to the church, but there was no church building to call home. Until we could purchase a place of our own, we met in a tiny church out in the country on Sunday nights. The folks who owned the building were nice enough to let us use their facility at no cost, but both parties understood this was only a temporary arrangement. The expectation was that we would be moving into a church building we'd signed a purchase contract on earlier that summer; however, the closing kept being postponed until finally, on the Monday before Thanksgiving, more than three months after we had arrived in Utica, the deal died.

With no building, no prospects for a building, and a holiday weekend starting in two days, I got into my car and started driving around the area, looking for any churches or buildings that might be for sale or available for rent. A couple of hours into my search I saw an old, dilapidated church building in the village of New York Mills with a sign that read "Community Center." I stopped to check it out, but the door was locked. I walked across the street to the courthouse, introduced myself to the town clerk, and asked her, "I noticed the community center across the street, and I was wondering if you would consider renting it on Sundays."

The clerk's eyes opened wide, and her exact words were, "We've never rented the building, but would you be interested in buying it?"

Over the next ten months we purchased and restored the building and spread the word that we'd be holding our first public worship service on the Sunday after Labor Day 2002.

Once we opened, attendance began to increase rapidly. In nine months we doubled in size, and after another nine months we'd doubled in size again. It was March 2004—just a year and a half after we'd begun holding services in our new location—and there were nearly 350 people attending our Sunday services. For those of you accustomed to big churches, 350 people may not sound like a lot, but in a community where churches are struggling to survive, a growing congregation of 350 people is a crowd.

To be honest, I had mixed emotions about the whole thing. It was nice that the church was growing, but most of the growth was due to people changing churches, and most of those people were there to consume a "safe place" rather than to help create a "safe place." As I saw it, the vision was in jeopardy, and we needed a watershed moment that would define our future. So I decided to do a two-week sermon series titled "A Look at Our Future." In the second sermon, The Good News, I was planning to talk about the incredible opportunity we had to make a difference in the lives of people in central New York. The vision centered on buying land and constructing a large church facility that would function as our hub for equipping people to go out and serve their communities. The vision also included converting our current facility back into a community center and over time buying other churches throughout the region, forming a network of community centers. By centralizing church programs in one location, we could then dedicate more time and resources to serving people. Each community center would tailor its programs to the needs of the local community. I dreamed of day care programs, after-school tutoring, food banks, clothing banks, homeless housing, and other services for families. How awesome would it be to convert struggling and dying churches into life-giving community centers? That's "creating a safe-environment for experiencing God-centered life change." That's regaining perspective on what really matters in life.

I was excited about the potential future of our church, and I looked forward to preaching The Good News, but first I felt compelled to offer a sober assessment of where we stood.

On March 7, 2004, I preached The Bad News.

I began the sermon by reminding the congregation that as Christians we are called to give our lives to Christ—nothing more and nothing less.

Then, I turned to the Old Testament book of Malachi. The book was written as a response to the grumblings of the Israelites at a time when they believed God had abandoned them. In short, God was angry with the Israelites because they'd begun to doubt his love for them, and because they doubted his love, they'd stopped trusting him as the Sustainer of life.

Based on the Law God had given Moses, the Israelites were supposed to express their trust in God by making animal sacrifices with the best of their flocks and herds. Instead, however, the Israelites were sacrificing their blind, crippled, and diseased animals. What made matters worse was that the Israelites didn't understand why God was displeased with their lame offerings. Offended by their worthless sacrifices, God stated that he would rather somebody shut the temple door than continue lighting useless fires on the altar. The book of Malachi ends with God threatening the Israelites, saying that they had to change their ways, "or else I will come and strike the land with a curse."

In turning to Malachi, I compared the Israelite community to our church community. I mentioned how many Christians in central New York were like the Israelites during the time of Malachi, feeling as though God had abandoned them. I made ten comparisons between what the Israelites had done and what we'd been doing as a church. I explained that we were not trusting God as the Sustainer of life because we were giving God our leftover time, money, and resources, and that God was not pleased with our lame offerings. I continued by saying that God would rather we close our doors than continue giving him less than our best, fooling ourselves into thinking what we were doing was somehow good and pleasing to God.

I ended the sermon with a minute of silence so people could reflect on the message. Then I closed the service on my knees and offered the following prayer:

> Father, in the book of Malachi you tell us, "cursed is the cheat who has an acceptable male in his flock and vows to give it but then sacrifices a blemished animal to the Lord, for I am a great king says the Lord Almighty and my name is to be feared among the nations."
>
> Father, on behalf of our church body I confess our unfaithfulness to you. Father, forgive us for not thinking you care about Upstate New York. Forgive us for questioning your love for us. Forgive us for blaming you when things go wrong. Forgive us for questioning your will. Forgive us for complaining and being ungrateful. And Father, forgive us for rationalizing our unfaithfulness.
>
> Father, forgive us that we do not carry our cross, that we are afraid to do so, and that we lose sight of the fact that nothing else matters than the glory of your Son. And I beg you, Father—continue to be patient with us, continue to bear with us, and may we at least be honest with you as we grapple with trying to be faithful. Father, you have blessed us so richly, thank you. And may we become the church that you desire us to become—for your glory. And whether it's fifty of us or five thousand of us, may we follow hard after you, that you will be pleased with the worship and the lives we put before you!
>
> For the sake of your kingdom and for the glory of your Son we pray. Amen.

My hope was that our people would respond by trusting God more intensely than they'd ever done before. I was praying this would be the watershed moment that would set the stage for The Good News and the future of our church. I wanted us to make a significant impact in the Mohawk Valley, bringing hope and love to the many people in need.

But that's not what happened.

In the days after I shared The Bad News, the chatter began: Cornerstone Community Church was no longer a "safe" place. My sermon had apparently been too confrontational, and the word on the street was that I was becoming a tyrant. The following week, when I delivered The Good News, there was not as much excitement about the vision for our future as I'd hoped there would be.

In the months that followed things got … rough. And it wasn't just fallout from The Bad News sermon; there were other issues and interpersonal tensions that had been brewing for some time that finally had come to a head.

In June 2004, something unexpected but inevitable happened: I could no longer control the chaos or manage my anxiety, and I broke down. The anxiety I experienced was so debilitating that getting out of bed became a daily struggle, and for much of the next year it was difficult for me to function. If you were to have put a scarf, a can of WD-40, and a fork in front of me and asked me to put them away, I would've shut down, not knowing where to begin. The decision of which one to put away first would have been too overwhelming for me.

"What happened? What went wrong?" I kept asking myself.

The truth was: I needed perspective. I thought I was living in God's T; little did I know the extent to which I was living in my T. And even though I should have known better, having been teaching Genesis 3 for several years, I started to blame God for sending me to the cursed lands of central New York, and I started to blame the people who'd cursed my name and abandoned me. I didn't want to concede the fact that I had no one to blame for my breakdown except myself, so I became "that guy," employing one blame-game strategy after another, trying to maintain the illusion of control.

You see, when life is working, it's easy to think you're living in God's T, and when you're so blessed that it doesn't hurt to give away some of your time, money, and resources, it's easy to think you're offering God your best. But when the illusion of control vanishes and your T begins to crumble, that's when you either trust God as the Sustainer of life or you play the blame game to preserve your own existence. That, my friends, is where the rubber meets the chicken.

CHAPTER 7

≈

NO PAIN, NO GAIN

¹⁶To the woman he said, "I will greatly increase your pains in childbearing; with pain you will give birth to children."

—Genesis 3:16a

ONCE GOD ASSERTED his authority in the garden of Eden, Adam and Eve were nearly speechless. In fact, we don't hear another peep from Adam, and Eve had just one last thing to say. We find Eve's final words at the start of the next chapter. Genesis 4 begins: "Adam lay with his wife Eve, and she became pregnant and gave birth to Cain. She said, 'With the help of the Lord I have brought forth a man.'"

The last recorded words of Adam and Eve in the Bible are Eve saying, "With the help of the Lord I have brought forth a man." In this brief statement Eve recognized her need for God's help as well as God's presence in childbirth. With great pain in childbearing, Eve gained perspective that God is the Giver of life. God gave women difficulty in childbearing and cursed the ground and the animals so through the pain of life and death we would gain perspective that God alone is the Giver and Sustainer of life.

Although I, as a man, cannot directly experience the pain of childbirth, I find the difficulty of childbearing more troublesome than the curse on the land and the animals. If it wasn't for modern medicine, my sister would have died from an abnormal pregnancy, and my wife might have died during childbirth.

The complications of my wife's first pregnancy began months before the birth itself. An ultrasound revealed the baby was in a breech position. The doctor was not concerned, but he wanted to monitor the situation with regular ultrasounds. He said that the baby would probably flip on its own, but if it didn't he would try to turn it.

Turn it? How would he turn it?

As luck would have it, the baby didn't flip, and a week or two before Anne-Marie's due date, we went to the delivery ward of the hospital so the doctor could *turn* the baby. The procedure was called an aversion. What the doctor did was use an ultrasound to determine the exact position of the baby, and then he put his hands on my wife's abdomen and pushed in with his fingers until he could feel the baby's head with one hand and the baby's bottom with the other. He then pushed down on the head and up on the bottom and turned the baby. It was bizarre and amazing at the same time. I could not believe how far he'd pushed his fingers into my wife's abdomen, and seeing the baby turn was unreal.

The baby flipped without any problems, but we had to stay in the hospital for a few hours so the nurses could monitor the baby's stress level and be sure that the aversion hadn't induced labor and that the umbilical cord had not become wrapped around the baby's neck. Fortunately the procedure was successful, and a few hours later we went home.

Over the next few weeks Anne-Marie experienced some contractions, and we had a couple of false alarms. As luck would have it, the false alarms came in the middle of the night, so Anne-Marie was not getting enough sleep, and she was very tired. One morning I woke up and found her on the couch, sitting uncomfortably. She had been up since 2:00 a.m., "napping" between contractions. We had an appointment with her doctor that afternoon, so we stayed home until then.

When we met with the doctor, he said that Anne-Marie was not ready to be admitted but that we should return to the hospital the next morning regardless of how her contractions were progressing because, if necessary, he would administer medication to induce labor. In other words, ready or not, we were going to have a baby.

Over the course of that day Anne-Marie continued having contractions. They were hitting her every ten to fifteen minutes, so she was unable to sleep that afternoon, that evening, and that entire night.

Six o'clock the next morning—twenty-eight hours after her contractions had begun—it was time to go to the hospital. However, before we left I did what only "that guy" would do—I pulled out my video camera and asked my wife if there was anything she wanted to say. Quietly, she uttered, "I'm ready for this to be over. It has been very hard."

When we arrived at the hospital, I walked Anne-Marie to the delivery ward and got her situated in her room. She put on one of those sweet hospital gowns, and I helped her climb into bed.

My wife was ready for the ordeal to be over, but it had barely even started—the nurse that examined her told us that she was at only two centimeters. For those of you who've been through this, you know what that means. For those of you who haven't, all you need to know is that my wife's body was not even close to the point of giving birth.

A nurse gave her medication to induce labor, but that made things only worse. The contractions hit harder and lasted longer, but my wife's body was not responding—she was still at two centimeters. Anne-Marie was in excruciating pain, and when the nurse tried to dismiss her screams, saying that she had "no reason" to feel pain between contractions, my wife—a kind and gentle person—lost it!

After giving the nurse an earful, Anne-Marie started to cry. She was scared, she was exhausted, and she just wanted it to be over, but at two centimeters she still had a long way to go.

At that moment, if you had given Anne-Marie the choice between God's help and an epidural, I promise you she would have taken the epidural, and I would have supported her in that decision. I know that by doing theological gymnastics we can avoid that choice by just thanking God for the epidural. Yet honestly, in that moment all she wanted was for the pain of childbirth to go away. After thirty hours of labor and praying for God's help, my wife was crying for an epidural, and I wanted her to have it.

About an hour later the greatest of all superheroes—Epidural Man—arrived to administer the drugs. Thank God.

I had to wait outside the room while they did the procedure. When I came back in, my wife was smiling and in no pain, and she fell asleep.

Thirty minutes into her nap the nurse told me that I had to wake her up.

What? Wake her up?

Apparently, in the half hour that she'd been asleep, she'd gone from two centimeters to ten centimeters, and it was time to start pushing. Thirty-two hours into labor, and now it was time to start pushing?

For the next two hours I lied to my wife like it was my job. I kept telling her that she was almost there and that if she just pushed a few more times the baby would come out. I had no idea what I was talking about. I'd never been through anything like this before, and I really didn't think it was going to take two hours of pushing. Near the end, the nurses looked a little nervous, and there seemed to be too many of them around, but I didn't have time to ask what was going on—I was too busy lying to my wife.

Finally, after thirty-four hours of labor, at 3:18 p.m. on March 5, 2002, Kirstin Karen Hayduchok was born. With the help of God and modern medicine my wife brought forth a child.

I thank God for modern medicine. I thank God the doctor was able to turn Kirstin so she was not born breech. I thank God for the epidural. I thank God for giving my wife the strength to survive the birth.

But what if it had been a hundred years ago? What if we had lived where there was no modern medicine? Kirstin would have come out breech, and she and/or my wife might have died in the process. As it was, they were close to calling for a C-section because Anne-Marie was on the brink of exhaustion and the baby was stressed and needed to come out.

What if my wife had died? What if my baby had died? How would that have changed my perspective on life?

What if your wife died? Or your baby died? Or your mother died? How would that change your perspective on life?

Would we gain a greater appreciation for God's help in childbearing?

Would we regain perspective that God is the Giver of life?

———

In every culture there are certain questions people ask that have a "right" answer. For example, when a woman spends two hours getting ready to go out to dinner with her husband and asks him, "How do I look?" every married man in America, and maybe the world, knows there is a right answer to that question.

Questions with right answers reflect the values of a culture. The degree to which a woman needs to look pretty before going out on a date communicates the degree of importance that culture places on physical beauty.

I make this observation about certain questions having right answers because in American culture, particularly in suburban culture, there's one question with a right answer that speaks volumes about how we view life and our children. When an expecting parent is asked, "Do you want a boy or a girl?" there are communities where the right answer is, "It doesn't matter. We just want the baby to be healthy."

There wasn't always a right answer to this question. There was a time when parents could say, "We'd like a girl" or "We're hoping for a boy." But today, in the age of gender equality, it has become somewhat taboo for parents to prefer one gender over the other, especially when it is their first child. After the first child, parents are allowed to desire a same-gender sibling to be a perfect playmate or to "try for" the other gender. When it comes to a first child, however, if you're asked, "Do you want a boy or a girl?" the right answer in many parts of American society is, "It doesn't matter. We just want the baby to be healthy."

That answer sounds nice, doesn't it? Maybe even noble? "It doesn't matter. We just want the baby to be healthy." Those words sound so selfless, so loving, but are they?

When we say, "We just want the baby to be healthy," we'd like to think we're being altruistic—not wanting our children to struggle with an abnormality or disability. That's what we'd like to think, but I believe there's more to it than that. I believe there's another reason why we want our children to be healthy—a reason we'd rather not recognize or admit.

My sister-in-law, Karen, has Down syndrome. Karen is a healthy, happy woman who'd probably make you smile if you met her. And Karen is not alone in this; as a whole, people with Down syndrome are some of the friendliest, most pleasant people you'll ever meet. If individuals who have Down syndrome are even close to being as satisfied with life as they appear, then why, when given a prenatal diagnosis of Down syndrome, do 90 percent of women choose to abort their pregnancies?[36] Unless the vast majority of people with Down syndrome secretly wish they'd never been born, then women are not aborting fetuses out of selfless love for their child.

This brings us to the second seemingly altruistic reason for why we want our children to be healthy. The argument goes something like this: "We don't want to burden society with the time, money, and resources needed to care for those who cannot care for themselves." If we accept this line of reasoning, then the door is open to euthanizing anyone who's not a contributing member of society. Baby boomers, who once championed this argument in support of aborting unwanted pregnancies, seem to be less comfortable with the concept of euthanasia as they are getting older, realizing that they will not always be able to care for themselves and that the overwhelming number of them will eventually become a burden on society.

Please don't hear those last two paragraphs as a pro-life rant; the point I'm making runs deeper than that. What I am bringing to light are the implications of a society that has lost sight of God as the Giver of life.

In today's world we don't view the "miracle of life" as being much of a miracle anymore. The microscope has allowed us to unravel the mystery of conception, the pill and abortion have given women power over pregnancy, anesthesia has reduced the pain of childbirth, and modern prenatal and postnatal care have greatly reduced the mortality rates of mother and child. Thanks to modern medicine we have essentially gained control over pregnancy and childbirth, and having done so we no longer need to view God as the Giver of life. Now we can see ourselves as the givers of life, and we can feel justified in deciding when life begins and when life should end.

Seeing ourselves as the givers of life has significant implications for how we view our children. Instead of viewing them as being created in "the image of God," we view them as being created in our image. Instead of teaching our children to pursue what God created them to be, we encourage them to be whatever they want to be, and we push and manipulate them to do what we want them to do.

Yes, we want our children to be healthy for their benefit, but we also want them to be healthy for our benefit. A healthy child makes a more flattering accessory for a mannequin on display than a child who is deformed, handicapped, or retarded.

If you think I'm being too harsh or overstating my point, consider the ultimate goal of the Human Genome Project. We want to think the goal of mapping human DNA is to eradicate disease and birth defects. That may be a goal, but is it *the* goal? I think the ultimate goal is immortality. As the givers of life we want the ability to give ourselves eternal life, and if we cannot make ourselves immortal, then the second-best option is to have the ability to create our children in whatever image we desire. If we can successfully identify, reproduce, and splice all the genes needed to form a human being, maybe we can fashion the idols of our dreams. Can you imagine a build-a-baby boutique where we could flip through catalogues of human traits, from eye color to IQ, custom designing our children, with the only limitation being the balance in our checking account?

Whether we want to believe it or not, this is where we are trying to take technology in the twenty-first century. Although God told Adam, "for dust you are and to dust you will return," we are unwilling to accept God as the Giver and Sustainer of life—we want to give ourselves eternal life.

As technology continues to advance in the twenty-first century, offering us more and more control over pregnancy and childbirth, who or what will we trust as the giver of life? Will we spend more time pursuing ageless immortality? Will we commit more energy to living like mannequins on display? Will we try to fashion our children into the idols of our dreams? Or will we become more grateful for the life we have, embrace the limits of our humanity, and love our children as God created them?

~

When the Giver of life created me, He chose to make me goofy—I was born left handed.

One little-known, fun fact about left-handed people is that we have a knack for spotting other left-handed people. It's not that we walk around searching for one another; it's that left-handed people tend to notice when someone else is eating, writing, or throwing with his or her left hand. Sometimes we'll even go out of our way to make a comment or exchange a few words with a fellow lefty.

It may seem odd—left-handed people noticing other left-handed people—but it's a social phenomenon. When you're born different from a societal norm, you develop an unspoken camaraderie with those who share your kind of different, and you tend to spot one another, especially if your kind of different is culturally frowned upon.

For me, as a Ukrainian-American, I had the pleasure of experiencing my kind of different in two cultures. As luck would have it, one culture accepted my kind of different while the other did not.

American society, being an informal culture, does not shun or discriminate against left-handed people. In fact, Americans encourage their young to develop fine motor skills with whichever hand they prefer. If a child wants to eat with his or her left hand, that's fine—American parents don't care; they just want their children to learn how to eat without shoveling food up their noses.

In contrast to American society, Ukrainian society is a formal culture in which using one's left hand to perform civilized tasks is considered uncouth. Any well-mannered Ukrainian will tell you there are simply some things you don't do with your left hand; a Ukrainian would never ever eat or write with the left hand. How uncivilized! How barbaric!

You might think this clash in cultures presented a problem or created some degree of confusion for me and my family, but it didn't. There was no problem and there was certainly no confusion. It was perfectly clear: my parents were emigrants from Ukraine, which meant our family was Ukrainian, which meant we honored the etiquette of Ukrainian culture, which meant I had to do things the "proper" way, which meant I was not allowed to write or eat with my left hand. There was no debate, no discussion, and most certainly no confusion.

Given the importance my parents placed on doing things the "proper" way, you can imagine my surprise when one day my mother gave me permission to write with my left hand. I was shocked. I could hardly believe it. What changed in the world of proper that suddenly made it okay for me to start using my left hand? I so wanted to ask that question, but of course I couldn't. That would be like a criminal serving a life sentence being released from prison and on his way out stopping by the warden's office to ask, "Why are you letting me go?" When something so wonderfully unexpected goes your way, you just smile and quietly move along before the arbiters of good and evil change their minds.

Thirty years later I have yet to receive an explanation for why I was released from left-handed prison. The closest my mother has ever come to telling me occurred during a conversation we had a few years after Kirstin was born. I was asking my mother questions about raising children when she went out of her way to tell me that one of the few regrets she had in raising her children was forcing me to be right-handed. Wow! I was not expecting to hear that. Then my mother said that she was convinced that making me write with my right hand was the cause of my stuttering problem and she wished that she had done things differently. Wow! I really was not expecting to hear that.

At that point I could have asked my mother what had transpired that made it okay for me to start using my left hand, but honestly I didn't think it mattered anymore. Over time I came to understand my parents' worldview and accept what was expected of me.

It was not until I experienced my breakdown and started meeting with a counselor that I began to understand the depth to which my identity was shaped by needing to do things the "proper" way. The most important self-discovery I made came during a session when my counselor asked me something along these lines: "Leon, if you took away everybody's expectations of you—what your parents expect you to do, what your wife expects you to do, what your parishioners expect you to do, even what you think God expects you to do—what is it that *you* want to do?"

I, being the "good" Christian pastor I was, objected to the question, saying something like, "What do you mean what do I want to do? That's a selfish thing to think. It's not about what I want to do. It's about being faithful to what I'm supposed to do."

I'm not sure exactly the words my counselor spoke after that, but it roughly translated to this: "Leon, stop the bullshit. I know you better than that, and we both know that you want to do what's right. So stop avoiding the question and tell me: what is it that *you* want to do?"

I had no idea. I had no idea what I wanted to do. So I just sat there mulling over the question until I started to cry.

I wasn't crying because I was sad. They weren't tears of pain; they were tears of relief. For the first time I was thinking about what I wanted to do—what I was created to do—without being distracted by the noise of expectations in my head. Instead of feeling the pressure to perform, I started feeling the freedom to be what the Giver of life created me to be.

For as long as I could remember I'd felt as though I had to do things the "proper" way, and I was afraid to make a mistake. Whenever I did make a mistake, I played the blame game, always having a reason or an excuse for not being perfect. I didn't want to disappoint my parents or bring shame upon my family, and I certainly didn't want to disappoint God or bring shame upon the church.

I had no idea the extent to which I'd been living like a mannequin on display. I'd been trying so hard to meet what I thought were everybody's expectations of me, even God's expectations of me, that I wasn't free to be myself or to make mistakes. I wasn't free to be human.

The truth is I needed perspective. Before the breakdown I was working seven days a week, answering my cell phone every time it rang, and saying yes to nearly every request made of me. I was so focused on being "all things to all people" that I wasn't allowing myself to be the person I was created to be.

It's been eight years since I had my breakdown—eight years of discovering and dealing with my relational issues and perfectionist tendencies. It's been a difficult journey, but as I wrote in chapter 3, I don't want to live like a mannequin on display with a lifeless smile, void of inner consciousness and feeling. I want to feel the passion and emotion that come with being human. And if that means I have to experience the shame, pain, and sadness of death in order to experience the joy, wonder, and love of life, so be it.

I want to be who the Giver of life created me to be. I want to live naked and unashamed.

A little over a year ago my mother moved into an elder-care facility. Because she has dementia and suffers from its complications, she has her good days and her bad days. When I visit her on a bad day she struggles to recognize me, but when I catch her on a good day she can describe in detail the moment I was born. When I'm with her and she's feeling well, we reminisce about the days when I was her little Levchik, and we recite the Ukrainian nursery rhymes she whispered to me back when she tucked me into bed.

On those good days my mother always asks, "How are the girls?" She loves to hear about her grandchildren. She wants to know how old they are, how big they are, and what activities they're involved in. Sometimes she repeats a question I'd answered a few minutes earlier, but that's okay. What father gets tired of talking about his children?

On my most recent visit I arrived shortly before dinner. I was sitting with my mother, telling her about my girls, when the nurse arrived with her meal. I helped my mother climb into bed, and I placed her tray of food in front of her.

Can you guess what happened next?

My mother picked up her fork and started eating with her left hand.

My mother is a fellow lefty. After more than seventy-five years of eating with her right hand, my mother in the later stage of her life is either no longer aware of or does not care about what is "proper"—she was eating with her left hand. For the next six days I sat and visited with my mother, and every time a meal came, I watched her pick up her fork and eat with her left hand. After seventy-five years my mother had finally given herself permission to be who God created her to be.

I didn't think it mattered anymore—why I'd been given permission to use my left hand—but as I sat with my mother during this visit, I figured out what must have happened. And do you know what? It does matter.

My mother stood up for me. My mother fought to give me the opportunity she'd never been given—the opportunity to be who I was created to be.

I thank God for my mother and for the strength he has given her. I also thank God for the perspective I'm starting to gain.

CHAPTER 8

~

THE FIGHT FOR CONTROL

Your desire will be for your husband, and he will
rule over you.

—Genesis 3:16b

IN THE MIDST of proclaiming a curse on the animals and the
ground and greatly increasing the pain of childbearing, God said
to the woman, "Your desire will be for your husband, and he will
rule over you." What do these words mean exactly? What is God
saying in this cryptic statement?

Well, that depends on whether this statement is part of God's
judgment upon the woman for eating the forbidden fruit or whether
God is describing the natural consequences of humankind having
acquired the knowledge of good and evil.

If this statement is part of the woman's punishment, then God is
proclaiming that the woman's desire should be to please her husband
and that she is to submit to his rule. However, if this statement is
not part of the woman's punishment—if God instead is describing
human nature—then the intended meaning of "Your desire will
be for your husband, and he will rule over you" depends on the
definition of the words "desire" and "rule."

The Hebrew word translated as "desire" can be interpreted with either a positive or a negative connotation. Interpreted positively, the woman's desire would be a yearning to experience oneness and intimacy with her husband. Interpreted negatively, the woman's desire would be a craving to dominate in her relationship with her husband. So which one is it? If God is describing human nature, then is God saying the woman's desire will be to love her husband or to control her husband?

Likewise, the Hebrew word translated as "rule" can also be interpreted with either a positive or a negative connotation. Interpreted positively, the man's rule would convey his responsibility to care for and oversee the well-being of his wife. Interpreted negatively, the man's rule would suggest an overbearing dominance in which the man does everything in his power to subjugate his wife. So which one is it? If God is describing human nature, then is man's rule over his wife God's declaration of male headship or God's prediction of female oppression?

Despite the ambiguity of these words, the long-standing Judeo-Christian tradition has been to view this statement as part of God's judgment upon the woman. It was not until the twentieth century, until the emergence of feminist theology, that the interpretation of this cryptic pronouncement began to come into serious question.

For thousands of years, under the guise of faith and tradition, it has been convenient for religious systems ruled by men to interpret these words as being the woman's punishment for eating the forbidden fruit and leading the man astray. In societies around the world, this interpretation has contributed to man's stranglehold over woman and justified cultural practices that allow women to be viewed and treated like property.

Given how men have historically dishonored women, is it any wonder why the traditional interpretation of "Your desire will be for your husband, and he will rule over you" would be questioned by the women's movement? Rather than interpreting this statement as God's judgment, those seeking equal rights for women have argued for an interpretation by which God is describing human nature using "desire" with a positive connotation and "rule" with a negative connotation. This liberal interpretation would paraphrase God's statement as follows: the woman will desire to experience intimacy with her husband, but the husband will rule his wife with an iron fist.

In response to feminist theology, conservative theologians have either continued to defend the punishment interpretation or have argued for an interpretation in which God is describing human nature using "desire" with a negative connotation and "rule" with a positive connotation. This conservative interpretation would paraphrase God's statement as follows: the woman will desire to usurp her husband's authority even though God has instructed her to submit to his rule.

Which is it? Which interpretation is correct?

Before you decide, I'd like to present one additional possibility. The following interpretation is not widely held, and supporting this position will not win you a lot of friends in either the liberal or conservative camps. It is an interpretation in which God is describing human nature using both "desire" and "rule" with negative connotations. This interpretation would paraphrase God's statement as follows: the woman will seek to control her husband, while the man will do whatever he can to control his wife.

Although this interpretation is not popular, it appears to me to be the best fit for the story. It's not as if either Adam or Eve was an innocent bystander. They both decided to trust in their own understanding, they both ate the fruit from the Tree of Knowledge of Good and Evil, and they both began to see themselves as arbiters of good and evil. Seeing the world from their own Ts, Adam and Eve were unwilling to submit to God; do you think either of them had any interest in submitting to the other? They both began living in a world according to me—a world in which "nobody has the right to tell me what to do!" The moment Adam and Eve ate the forbidden fruit, they took control of their own destinies—or so they thought.

By cursing the ground and animals and increasing the pain of childbirth, God was making it clear to Adam and Eve that they were not in control of their lives. By stating "Your desire will be for your husband, and he will rule over you," it appears that God was also saying that no matter how hard they tried they wouldn't be able to control each other's lives either.

If I'm correct, then God's observation may extend beyond the marital relationship; it may be a commentary on all human relationships. The story of Adam and Eve began as a love story in which God created the woman as the perfect companion for the man, and the two were supposed to experience oneness forever. If any two people on the planet should have been able to get along, it should have been Adam and Eve. For God to say that the woman will want to control her husband and that the man will want to control his wife suggests that God is announcing that all human relationships are at risk as we fight one another for control.

The more I think about it, the more I wonder if God's statement to the woman was intentionally cryptic. The abusive use of this verse and the debate over its meaning may be proving God's point. In a dramatic display of irony, the fight between liberals and conservatives over the interpretation of "Your desire will be for your husband, and he will rule over you" may have less to do with the fight for truth and more to do with the fight for control.

Have you ever been to a creation vs. evolution debate? In the late twentieth century these spectacles were the heavyweight bouts of America's culture war. I was lucky enough to attend one of these epic battles back in 1991. The fight was held in a performing arts auditorium at a prestigious liberal arts university. The event was sold out, but fortunately, being from New Jersey, I knew a guy.

The venue was packed and the crowd went wild when the two opponents were introduced. The man in the red corner, representing the young-earth creationists, had the swagger of a condescending Christian. The man in the blue corner, representing the evolutionists, had the look of an angry atheist. The place was raw with emotion, and when the two combatants met in the middle of the stage to shake hands, you could tell this was going to be one hell of a fight.

From the opening bell the evolutionist threw his hardest scientific data at the creationist, but the creationist was able to dodge and deflect most of the punches with theistic responses and anecdotal evidence that illustrated the uncertainty of evolutionary science. With each passing round the evolutionist grew more and more frustrated with the creationist's defense: unless the evolutionist could recreate the Big Bang or form life out of primordial soup, the creationist was not going to throw in the towel; he was not going to concede that the earth was billions of years old or that evolution was a scientific fact.

Unlike the evolutionist, the creationist didn't deliver hard, scientific punches. He seemed content to jab at his opponent, exposing the various gaps in the theory of evolution. The hardest scientific data he threw supported the biblical account of a worldwide flood, but it was not much of a punch. Some might have even called it a slap in the face of science.

After more than two hours of debating, neither man showed any signs of tiring, and neither one had the proof to land a knockout punch. As they stood there toe-to-toe, exchanging blows, the final bell rang, and the moderator stepped in to call an end to the fight. The debate was over.

So who won?

Well, it depends on whom you ask. There were no judges, so there was no official decision. When the moderator said good night and the house lights came on, it was time for everyone to leave, but the fight was far from over. As the crowd made its way up the aisles and out the front doors, so did the debate over who won, and no one was going to step in to stop that fight.

In the end I don't know if there were any winners in the creation vs. evolution debate, but I can tell you this: there are plenty of angry and condescending people in both camps who insist they're wearing the title belt of truth.

Truth? Is that what this was about? Was America's culture war a fight for truth? Did the creation vs. evolution debate devolve into a verbal street brawl because people were passionate about the truth? In hindsight I don't think so. There was a time when I believed in the fight for truth, but not anymore.

Truth—absolute truth—is not something that can be won or lost in a debate. Whether I think life on earth is a product of God's creation, evolution, alien invasion, or something else does not affect the truth. The truth is simply that—the truth. It is what it is.

Those involved in the creation vs. evolution debate can insist they're engaged in a noble fight for truth, but it's hard to see the endless debate as anything more than a shameless struggle for control. Regardless of what scientific data is brought forward, creationists refuse to give up the "good" fight, praying they'll win so they can bring creationism back into our public schools. Meanwhile, the evolutionists are just as committed to winning so they can keep creationism (i.e., religion) out of our public schools. Each camp passionately professes to be fighting for the truth, but the prize for winning the creation vs. evolution debate is not the belt of truth. The prize for winning the debate is control over what is printed in textbooks and taught to our children. When you strip away all the hoopla and posturing, the creation vs. evolution debate, like any other debate, is merely a fight to gain control over what is perceived and what is portrayed as the truth.

You see, we mistake the fight for control for the fight for truth when we presume that our perception of the truth—our knowledge of good and evil—is the truth. When we're convinced our T is the truth, we fight for our T, forming alliances with those who have similar Ts, with the goal of gaining control. If we can influence enough people or the right people in positions of power, then practically speaking we can control what is portrayed as the truth.

Please don't misunderstand me; I'm not saying truth is relative. Again, the truth is the truth. What I'm saying is that human beings have only a relative understanding of the truth, and it is important for us to acknowledge our biases and accept the limitations of our knowledge.

I'm an educated, white, male Ukrainian-American from New Jersey—that is who I am. No matter how hard I try, I can never see the world the way a black man, a woman, or a starving child in India sees it. Even when my T aligns with truth on any given subject, I still have only a limited understanding of that truth based on who I am and what I've experienced. To think I can transcend my whiteness, my maleness, or my life story and understand the fullness of truth is to guarantee my being blind to the white, male, privileged bias of my T. And when I'm blind to my whiteness, I'm racist; when I'm blind to my maleness, I'm sexist; when I'm blind to my privileged life, I'm classist.

Further, when we think our T is the truth, the whole truth, and nothing but the truth, we lose perspective—we begin to see ourselves as the givers and sustainers of life and as the arbiters of good and evil. When this happens, we cease to recognize we've been created in the image of God, and we start to create God in our image, thinking that our T *is* God's T.

Just consider what has happened to Christianity in the Western world. Because people like me—white men—have controlled the West, Western Christianity has literally portrayed Jesus as a white-skinned European man. Furthermore, because rugged, individualistic men control American culture, pasty-white American Jesus is a capitalist who helps those who first try to help themselves.

And please, in response to what I am writing, don't ask, "So is he suggesting we portray Jesus as an uneducated, black, homeless woman?" If you say that, you're not only missing my point but you're also blindly protecting your T.

When we are committed to living in a world according to me, we do whatever we can to protect our T. The more committed we are to our T, the more we become:

1. *Self-righteous* in that we believe we are always right and anyone who disagrees with us is either ignorant or just doesn't understand the "truth";

2. *Arrogant* in that we think other people don't have much knowledge to offer us, but we have plenty of knowledge to offer them;

3. *Unteachable* in that we are eager to learn more about what we already believe, not understanding that teachability is not a willingness to learn more but a willingness to think differently; and

4. *Bigoted* in that we believe our view of the world is *the* correct view of the world.

We all know people like this, right? People who have a reason or an excuse for every mistake they make; who prefer to talk rather than listen; who cannot get enough partisan "news," talk radio, or biblical teaching; and who are unable to relate to any problem or issue they have not personally experienced. You know people like this, right? People like Adam, Eve, you, and me.

The truth, at least as I understand it, is that we all have the knowledge of good and evil—we all have our own T—and therefore we all to some degree live in a world according to me. The problem with this is that it is a lot easier to see another person's T than to recognize our own. It reminds me of what Jesus said in his Sermon on the Mount: "Why do you look at the speck of sawdust in your brother's eye and pay no attention to the plank in your own eye?"

To tell you the truth, even though I've been thinking, studying, teaching, and writing about the garden of Eden drama and the Ts for more than thirteen years, I still need people in my life to help me see when I'm being "that guy"—the never-wrong, know-it-all, I'm better than you, punk from New Jersey.

To break free from the delusional world according to me, we need people in our lives who will expose our T and help us regain perspective—we need relationships that challenge us to see truth beyond the limits of who we are and what we've experienced—and we need to encourage each other to come out of hiding and help a world that is dying to control.

As technology continues to advance in the twenty-first century, offering us more and more knowledge, who or what will we recognize as the arbiter of good and evil? Will we feel more justified in doing what seems right in our own eyes? Will we spend more time gorging ourselves on forbidden fruit? Will we commit more energy to fighting for the best seats on the merryless-go-round? Or will we gain perspective on what is good and evil, share more of our good fortune with those in need, and stand up for those who have little to no voice?

Shortly after moving to central New York I met another pastor in town, Mike Ballman. Over time Mike and I developed a close friendship, and eventually we started working together. I asked Mike if he'd be willing to tell that story and explain what has happened at

Cornerstone Community Church since the day I preached The Bad News. He was kind enough to say yes.

Here's Mike.

Leon and I attended Dallas Theological Seminary together; however, since DTS is a fairly large seminary and I was three years ahead of him, we didn't actually know each other while we attended. Leon claims that a mutual acquaintance introduced us one afternoon, but I think that's a figment of his overactive imagination, as I don't remember meeting him. And, as anyone who has ever met Leon can attest, one does not forget the extravaganza that is meeting Leon.

Our first encounter was in the form of a phone conversation. I was pastoring a church in Utica, New York, and a mutual professor-friend of ours from seminary told me Leon had just been hired to pastor a new church in Utica and would be moving there soon. Knowing both of us well, he thought we'd hit it off. So I called Leon, and as advertised, I found him to be a "punk from New Jersey."

The thing about the conversation that tipped the "punk" scale for me was how he described the core group of the new church. As I shared with him the reality that there were no large or healthy evangelical churches in the area due to a long and pervasive history of church splits, doctrinal rivalries, and serial church hopping, he quickly interrupted me to state, "I don't think you know the people starting this church. We have some of most influential Christians in the area who have been the victims of these issues and are ready to be the first healthy church as a model for all the others."

As you can imagine, I was thinking "What's my church? Chopped liver? Who does this guy think he is?" Needless to say, after this conversation I wasn't looking forward to meeting Leon in person.

A few weeks later, after moving to Utica, Leon gave me a call, and we agreed to meet at a local diner to get acquainted. To my great surprise I learned an important universal constant, namely, Leon translates much better in person than on the phone. What I perceived as arrogance in our phone conversation, quite to the contrary in person, was a bold confidence in the message of Genesis 3 to help people have a more authentic experience with God. As he explained his concept of the Ts, in about an hour Leon helped me resolve my twenty-year nagging dissonance regarding the true nature of sin and salvation.

This dissonance had been nurtured in the finest of evangelical institutions. You see, I am an evangelical of evangelicals. I grew up as a fourth-generation staff member at a prominent Christian organization birthed from the revival movement at the turn of the twentieth century. I completed my undergraduate education at an evangelical Christian liberal arts college whose stated mission is to produce scholar servants with a Christian worldview. And I studied theology at a flagship evangelical seminary. One could argue that I had the best evangelical Christian education possible, but despite this great lineage, I really didn't understand why God would think someone like me was a sinner; thieves, murderers, liars, and fascist dictators I get, but not people like me. Intellectually I understood everyone is a sinner except Jesus, and since I'm not Jesus, I must be a sinner, but mostly I didn't feel like a sinner. Furthermore, I didn't have much conviction to tell other seemingly nice people that they were sinners too. And that was my dissonance with only the sin part.

The salvation message beaten into my head across all those great institutions also made little sense to me. It went something like this: once you realize you're a sinner (whatever that means), you must pray a salvation prayer—confess your sins and ask Jesus to be your personal Savior—and then you are forgiven of your sins. Consequently you will be so grateful that you will want to read your Bible every day, go to church three times a week, and tell everybody who's not an evangelical that they are sinners.

For evangelicals, this salvation message is all about having a "personal" relationship with Jesus, yet from my perspective it didn't seem very personal at all. The relationship begins with appeasing God with a formulaic prayer so he won't send you to hell, and then the relationship grows as you learn the Bible and stop committing the big sins (adultery, divorce, drinking, swearing, murder, etc.), all the while leading nonbelievers into this same relationship. That was the message I was taught across all those great evangelical institutions, which, arguably, is not bad. The implicit message, however, that accompanied the salvation message was what gave me indigestion: as long as you've prayed the right prayer of salvation, believe the evangelical doctrines, and don't commit any of the big sins, you're good with God no matter how much of an a-hole you may be.

So, yeah, saying that I had a nagging dissonance is actually an understatement, but unlike Leon, I have a compliant personality, so even though it all seemed hollow, vapid, and contrary to the Jesus I perceived from Scripture, I just thought the dissonance was my fault for not being disciplined enough to read the Bible, pray, and evangelize every day.

Leon was the first person who gave me a theological reason to say out loud what I really believed inside: the evangelical faith that had been handed down to me was deeply flawed in its understanding of sin and salvation. Ironically, while the evangelical message of salvation emphasizes the need for a personal relationship with God, it doesn't adequately explain the nature or essence of the God-man relationship—trust. We choose to have a relationship with God because we trust he is good and his ways are best for us, while sin is our desire to choose good and evil for ourselves and live independently of God. Framed in that perspective, I have no problem seeing the pervasiveness of my own sin and my need for God's forgiveness. Even better, this perspective closed the loopholes for many of the leaders and heroes of the evangelical world whom I had known who professed to have a personal relationship with God but still acted like a-holes.

Leon's take on Genesis 3 saved my faith.

From that point on we became very close friends and partners in ministry. For the first two years we supported each other by acting as sounding boards for one another with the day-to-day issues of our churches, writing sermons together, and playing a lot of pop-a-shot basketball. As time went on and Cornerstone grew, Leon hired me as an associate minister to keep up with the growth of the church.

That brings us up to the aforementioned Bad News sermon. Leon and I had come to the realization that many of the most influential members of our church were not in fact victims of the difficult local church culture but perpetrators of it. This in itself was not necessarily bad, as Cornerstone could have made a very positive statement to the other churches in the community if we as individuals and a church had recognized our part in the negative spiritual climate and had reached out to other churches in a spirit of repentance.

Unfortunately, things didn't go in that direction. Most people interpreted The Bad News sermon as a personal attack rather than an invitation to trust God and come out from behind the tree. Many took this invitation personally because they viewed the fractured and severed relationships from former churches as acceptable collateral damage in the name of fighting for truth. Consequently, they felt that Leon had some nerve to suggest that they might be complicit in the multiple church splits and closings that had plagued our community. Moreover, it wasn't just the church splitters and serial church hoppers who were offended;

this whole business about the motives of our hearts being as important to God as our verbal confession of faith made following God a lot harder than the dependable formula of praying the right prayer, practicing the right spiritual disciplines, and avoiding the "big" sins. After all, if you know how to act like a Christian mannequin on display, then you're bulletproof in the evangelical world, and why would anyone want to mess with that?

It was at this point that the church elders, Leon, and I began to reevaluate our priorities as a church. Catering to consumer Christians didn't seem so palatable anymore. We'd been spending most of our time and energy making sure our Sunday product included the most contemporary worship music, entertaining children's programs, and high-tech sermon presentations. Sure, we had a huge budget surplus every year, a growing congregation, and the local buzz as a "hip" church, but we were tired of the merryless-go-round of providing more and more religious products to a largely consumer audience. Worse yet, dealing with the constant unmet expectations of consumers who liked the product but were offended by the message crushed Leon emotionally and spiritually.

As Leon shared in chapter 6, he experienced a breakdown, and the debilitating anxiety made it difficult for him to work, but each week he at least managed to do what he does best—preach. So he kept preaching the message of trusting God as the Giver and Sustainer of life, while I took the lead in implementing the vision.

Yet what could we do? Cornerstone was conceived and constructed to be the first megachurch in our area—a beacon of light and a glorious vindication of the founding members to their misguided former congregations. So we did the only thing that made sense—the exact opposite of what we were doing. We called it "maximizing discontinuity."[37] Our intention wasn't to do a 180 just to be contrarian; we felt convicted that our founding values were, as Leon shared earlier, self-righteous, arrogant, unteachable, and bigoted. Everything we were doing to that point had allowed people to maintain their own T in their sheltered suburban world. We tried harder than ever to reach out to our neighbors near the church, but it was a close-knit community that really didn't need our help.

We needed something outside of ourselves to help us overcome our myopic perspective, but we didn't know where to start. Then one Sunday after church, one of our college students told me about an urban ministry in Utica he was involved in and asked me if I wanted to meet its director. Always eager to meet new people, I said sure. I met him at the facility later that week, and he introduced me to the founder and director of the ministry, Rev. Maria Scates.

To say that Reverend Scates is a charismatic personality is as understated as proposing that the sun is lukewarm. In a thirty-minute tour she affected me as greatly as Leon had with Genesis 3. In those short, few minutes she told me the story of how ten years earlier she'd felt called by God to show up in the most dangerous neighborhood in Utica and simply love her neighbors. She bought a burned-out house, fixed it up, provided a safe place for neighborhood kids to play and learn about God, worked with the city and community leaders to drive the drug dealers away, and improved the beauty and safety of the neighborhood. Within ten years she's rehabilitated several houses in that neighborhood to provide twenty-six apartments for a drug recovery program for women and their children. Utica is an immeasurably better place because Reverend Scates chose to love her neighbors. I couldn't help but feel a little embarrassed at seeing her accomplish all that on a shoestring budget while we racked up huge surpluses for entertaining rich people. Leon saved my faith, and Reverend Scates showed me what to do with it.

Over the next few years we began to help Reverend Scates with her youth and children's programs. It was stretching for us, but doing so allowed us to see the world beyond our church. For the first time many of us felt like we were doing something meaningful because Reverend Scates had invited us into a world that we had heretofore chosen to ignore.

Despite the incongruence between our sermons and the rest of the product we manufactured each week, our numbers had still grown enough that we needed a bigger facility. The plan all along had been to buy a huge parcel of land in the most affluent suburb of Utica and build a campus that would attract more suburban people. However, we really didn't want to be that kind of church anymore. So by God's grace a very different door opened for us. An aging urban mainline denominational church was looking for someone to buy its building on the condition that it could stay there rent-free until they eventually ran out of members. Even though we wanted to maximize discontinuity with our past, this was more discontinuity than we could ever have imagined. We set up an appointment to see the facility and were blown away by the beauty, capacity, and condition of the building. We were really sold on the reality that the asking price was far less than what it would have cost to build a new facility a quarter its size, yet the best part of it all was that it was only a few blocks from Reverend Scates's ministry.

The elders were all excited about the ministry possibilities of acquiring such a great facility with an entire floor for children's programming, a gymnasium, a huge game room, a commercial kitchen, and a large sanctuary. Did I mention the facility had a gymnasium? We presented the opportunity to the congregation for discussion. The small group of people who were involved in helping Reverend Scates regularly was supportive of the idea, but the rest of the church had some deep concerns. The primary concern was safety, which was code for "there are a lot of black people in that neighborhood." Several even contended in public meetings that to even consider moving to the city was irresponsible in its lack of concern for the safety of church families.

In hindsight, I wish I had named that concern the racism that it was, but I took the bait and presented a strong case for the statistical safety based on the current crime numbers of the neighborhood. However, the statistical reality that the neighborhood was indeed as safe as our suburban location didn't sway anyone, because safety wasn't the real issue.

Given the significant opposition, we tabled the purchase idea and took time to pray, reflect, and discern if moving to the city was the right move for us as a church. For the next six months Leon and I didn't raise the issue of relocating to the city to individual members or to the congregation as a whole. During this interval the elders found that they were even more committed to moving to the city, many of our congregants who opposed the move left the church, and the members of the church that owned the building were extremely accommodating to us. One year later we put our building up for sale and moved to the city.

The Genesis 3 deconstruction of our evangelical roots was complete; no more riding the merryless-go-round; no more pretty, plastic Christians living like mannequins on display; no more playing the blame game; and no more seeing the world through the lens of only "me." We were free to start building a new foundation based on love and trust, not fear and law.

That was five years ago. Today, Cornerstone is still flawed and imperfect, but now we're doing our best to bring those flaws out from behind the tree and into the open. Prostitutes, gang members, ex-cons, suburban dwellers, urban dwellers, and refugees from around the world all worship together on Sunday mornings in our banquet hall, around tables, facing one another as friends. And it's not just about gathering for church activities;

many of us from the suburbs have sold our houses and moved into the city so we can actively love our neighbors around the church by actually being neighbors.

Best of all, through all this we have experienced the reality that the greatest joy, meaning, and fulfillment in life comes from giving our lives away for the sake of loving others. Jesus' words have never meant more to us as a church: "For whoever wants to save their life will lose it, but whoever loses their life for me will save it."

CHAPTER 9

≈

FOR THE SHAME OF IT ALL

²⁰Adam named his wife Eve, because she would become the mother of all the living.

²¹The LORD God made garments of skin for Adam and his wife and clothed them.

²²And the LORD God said, "The man has now become like one of us, knowing good and evil. He must not be allowed to reach out his hand and take also from the tree of life and eat, and live forever."

²³So the LORD God banished him from the Garden of Eden to work the ground from which he had been taken.

²⁴After he drove the man out, he placed on the east side of the Garden of Eden cherubim and a flaming sword flashing back and forth to guard the way to the tree of life.

—Genesis 3:20–24

IN THE BEGINNING, when God created the heavens and the earth, he planted a garden in the east, in Eden, where he placed the man he had formed from the dust of the ground, and he gave the man permission to eat from any tree in the garden.

In the middle of the garden were two trees—the Tree of Life and the Tree of Knowledge of Good and Evil. Although the man was free to eat from any tree in the garden, God warned the man not to eat the fruit that hung on the Tree of Knowledge of Good and Evil, saying, "for when you eat of it you will surely die."

From the beginning, human beings have had the freedom to choose. The Tree of Life and the Tree of Knowledge of Good and Evil stand side by side at the heart of the garden of Eden drama, symbolizing the central question in the God-human personal relationship, "Do you trust me?"

Adam and Eve had a choice: they could either express their trust in God by eating from the Tree of Life, or they could trust in their own understanding by eating from the Tree of Knowledge of Good and Evil. It was their decision to make, and God gave them the freedom to make it.

Later, when the serpent—who "was more crafty than any of the wild animals the Lord God had made"—came onto the scene, he confused matters by splashing conflict all over the garden. Speaking to the woman about the Tree of Knowledge of Good and Evil, the serpent boldly proclaimed, "You will not surely die. For God knows that when you eat of it your eyes will be opened, and you will be like God, knowing good and evil." Overwhelmed with doubt, Eve was left to wonder whether God was a liar and whether God had her best interest in mind.

In the next scene of the drama, Adam and Eve chose to trust in their own understanding—they both ate the fruit that hung on the Tree of Knowledge of Good and Evil. Yet even though Adam and Eve ate the forbidden fruit, we, as the audience, are left to read and experience the rest of the story. We are left to decide for ourselves whether God is a liar and whether he has our best interest in mind.

So is God a liar?

When God warned Adam not to eat the fruit from the Tree of Knowledge of Good and Evil, God did not complicate the situation by explaining why or how death would occur. God kept it as simple as possible for the man, telling him, "you must not eat from the tree of the knowledge of good and evil, for when you eat of it you will surely die." God could not have presented the situation any more plainly than that to Adam.

However, when the serpent questioned Eve on whether she could eat fruit from the trees in the garden of Eden, Eve responded by saying, "God did say, 'You must not eat fruit from the tree that is in the middle of the garden, and you must not touch it, or you will die.'"

What? No! That's not what God said. God didn't say, "You must not touch it." Somewhere, somehow, somebody added something to God's prohibition.

We don't know whether Adam was "that guy" who was not paying attention when God was speaking to him or whether Adam told his wife, "Woman, come to think of it, don't even touch the fruit," or whether Eve was the first woman to make things more complicated than they actually were. We don't know. All we know is that Eve didn't rightly understand God's command; Eve thought that touching the forbidden fruit would result in death.

Do you know what happens when we alter or add to what God has said? We make God out to be a liar. Telling someone not to touch the forbidden fruit may create a hedge of protection around the Tree of Knowledge of Good and Evil, but it misrepresents God's word, and it opens the door to God being portrayed as a liar.

Realizing that the woman did not rightly understand God's command, the serpent took advantage of the situation, telling the woman, "You will not surely die. For God knows that when you eat of it your eyes will be opened, and you will be like God, knowing good and evil."

With the skill of a master magician, the serpent was able to redirect the woman's attention away from God's command and onto the fruit itself: "When the woman saw that the fruit of the tree was good for food and pleasing to the eye, and also desirable for gaining wisdom, she took some and ate it. She also gave some to her husband, who was with her, and he ate it."

What a crafty beast. Not only was the serpent able to redirect the woman's attention, but he was able to do it without lying. If you look closely at the story you'll see that the serpent was correct in telling Eve that eating the forbidden fruit would not kill her because the fruit itself was not lethal, and according to God's statement in Genesis 3:22, eating the forbidden fruit did make Adam and Eve like God, knowing good and evil.

In a sense the serpent was telling the truth, but then again so was God. Because Adam had acquired the knowledge of good and evil, "God banished him from the garden of Eden to work the ground from which he had been taken. After he drove the man out, he placed on the east side of the garden of Eden cherubim and a flaming sword flashing back and forth to guard the way to the tree of life." Outside the garden of Eden and cut off from the Tree of Life, Adam, just as God had said, would "surely die."

In the end, with death as an inevitable reality for Adam and Eve, it is fair to say that according to the garden of Eden drama, God is not a liar.

But does God have humankind's best interest in mind?

After God proclaimed the curse and before he banished Adam and Eve from the garden of Eden, there are two somewhat random—maybe even seemingly out of place—verses in Genesis 3.

The first of those two verses is Genesis 3:20: "Adam named his wife Eve, because she would become the mother of all the living." Looking at this verse within the context of the drama, two questions emerge. First, why does Adam name his wife when it was God who named Adam? Second, why is it that Eve receives her name as "the mother of all the living" so late in the story?

It is commonly believed, or maybe I should say that it was once generally accepted, that God, by giving Adam the honor of naming his wife, was making it clear a husband is to have authority over his wife. And as for why Eve is identified as "the mother of all the living" so late in the story, religious tradition teaches that the placement of this verse *after* Adam and Eve ate the fruit from the Tree of Knowledge of Good and Evil explains why all people, as descendants of Adam and Eve, are born with a sinful nature and why we must all endure the curse.

Whether or not you agree with the two positions in the above paragraph, I think it is fair to say that the garden of Eden drama, by identifying Eve as "the mother of all the living" *after* Adam and Eve had eaten the forbidden fruit and *after* the curse, suggests that all human beings are like Adam and Eve—each of us wants to live in a world according to me, according to my own T—and that the curses and the pain in childbirth present each of us with the opportunity to trust God as the Giver and Sustainer of life.

The second somewhat random verse between the curse and Adam and Eve being evicted from the garden of Eden is Genesis 3:21: "The LORD God made garments of skin for Adam and his wife and clothed them." God's final act before banishing Adam and Eve from the garden of Eden—God's parting gift to humanity—was ... a makeover? Really? Why?

If God has humankind's best interest in mind, then why replace fig leaves with fur? In our twenty-first-century world—a world flooded with tragedy and suffering—what do we gain from a wardrobe change?

If God has our best interest in mind, then the "garments of skin" he provided Adam and Eve were more than new outfits for mannequins on display. God's parting gift must in some fashion reflect his tireless pursuit of humankind, where he once again presents the essential, ever-present, unspoken question in the God-human personal relationship, "Do you trust me?"

I hope God is trustworthy.

I hope I answer, "Yes."

⌒

Do you ever feel ashamed?

If you're anything like me, then you may have said or done sometime this week or last Friday night you're not proud of, and you wish—oh, how you wish—it had never happened.

Assuming for a moment that you've done at least one shameful deed at some point in your life, let me ask you, what did you do with your shame? As Americans, how are we supposed to deal with our shame? In American society we don't have a social structure or a legal system that addresses shame. The United States is an innocence-guilt culture in which we emphasize personal integrity and individual responsibility. In our culture, it is important for individuals to maintain their innocence, which is why we teach our children it's never appropriate to lie, cheat, or steal. If someone gets caught breaking the law or has a moral failing that becomes public, that individual is declared guilty and needs to make some form of restitution. However, paying a fine or serving time doesn't address a person's shame. A rapist may pay for his guilt in prison, but on the day he's set free, how does he escape his shame? As for his victim, what is she supposed to do if she, after hearing the guilty verdict, exits the courtroom feeling naked and ashamed?

In contrast to American culture, most other societies around the world are honor-shame cultures that emphasize people's responsibility to their family and to their tribe, clan, or community. In these cultures it is important for people to maintain their collective honor, which is why they teach their children it's appropriate to do whatever is necessary to avoid bringing shame upon their people. If someone gets caught breaking the law or has a moral failing that becomes public, then that individual has not only brought shame upon himself but also upon his collective group, and he must seek to regain the lost honor. Regaining honor, however, can be difficult, and in some cultures, in extreme cases, the honorable thing to do is to commit suicide.

So again I ask, how are we supposed to deal with our shame?

Because American culture is so biased toward an innocence-guilt perspective on life, shame is not just an issue our society struggles to address; shame is an issue our society struggles to recognize. We Americans want to believe there is no reason to be ashamed of ourselves if we haven't committed a crime, but we don't have to be guilty of breaking the law to bring shame upon ourselves, our families, and our communities. Furthermore, because guilt and shame feel much the same, when we experience shame, we often mistake those feelings for guilt. Yet guilt and shame are not the same; guilt and shame reflect different offenses.

Unlike guilt, which is an emotion that individuals feel when they violate a law, shame is an emotion that an entire group feels when one of its members violates a relationship. Therefore, when we as human beings fail to treat one another with respect or when we break the bond of trust in a personal relationship, we bring shame upon ourselves, upon the relationship we violate, and upon the community of people we represent.

Take divorce, for example. It's legal to get divorced in the United States, and in many cases people get divorced because of irreconcilable differences—neither party was guilty of breaking the law or of having a moral failing. Yet regardless of the circumstances there is a certain degree of shame associated with any divorce, and that shame is felt not just by the two individuals involved—their children feel the shame, their extended family feels the shame, and their close friends feel the shame.

You see, in a divorce, two people who committed their lives to one another—"for better or for worse, till death do us part"—are formally severing a relationship that was intended to last forever, and everyone who shared in the joy and honor of their marriage also shares in the sorrow and shame of their divorce.

The point here is not that divorced people are guilty of breaking their vows or that divorced people should feel guilty for getting divorced. This is not about guilt and innocence; this is about shame and honor. And the point here is that any personal relationship that has been violated is a heartbreaking reality that brings shame upon both the individuals involved and everyone who feels connected to the offense.

As Americans, we may live with an innocence-guilt perspective on life, but as human beings we feel the shame of our violated relationships. We can suppress our shame, or we can try to address our shame as if it were guilt, but unlike guilt, we cannot pay for our shame. It doesn't matter how much or how often we pay, the shame we feel as lingering guilt cannot be paid away.

So once again I ask, how are we supposed to deal with our shame?

The garden of Eden drama speaks to the issue of shame; however, instead of interpreting the story from the perspective of honor and shame, Western Christianity has interpreted the story from the perspective of innocence and guilt. Hence, in American culture, the garden of Eden drama centers on the guilt of Adam and Eve and how God—the righteous Judge—punished them (and all humanity) for breaking the law.

Sure, Adam and Eve were guilty, but the garden of Eden drama originated in an honor-shame culture, and therefore the story draws the audience's attention to the honor and shame in the God-human personal relationship. We see this theme most clearly in verse 2:19, where God brings every living creature to Adam "to see what he would name them; and whatever the man called each living creature, that was its name." By giving Adam the privilege of naming the animals, God was honoring humankind above every living creature, which is why Genesis 2 fittingly ends with the words, "The man and his wife were both naked, and they felt no shame."

But then, when Adam and Eve ate the fruit from the Tree of Knowledge of Good and Evil, they broke their bond of trust with God, bringing shame upon themselves and their relationship with God. Feeling the shame of it all, Adam and Eve covered their naked bodies, and when they heard God walking in the garden of Eden, they hid from God among the trees in the garden.

From that point forward in the story God pursues Adam and Eve, looking to reconcile their relationship. By calling out to Adam, "Where are you?" and by speaking to both Adam and Eve directly, God was giving each of them the opportunity to confess to what they had done and to apologize. But instead of taking the path of reconciliation, Adam and Eve both chose to play the blame game.

Despite Adam and Eve's unwillingness to reconcile, God didn't give up on his relationship with humankind. Before evicting Adam and Eve from the garden of Eden, "The LORD God made garments of skin for Adam and his wife and clothed them."

By making garments for Adam and Eve, God was acknowledging the nakedness they were feeling; and by clothing them, God was addressing their shame. In his parting gift to Adam and Eve, God was reaching out yet again, saying in effect, "Trust me to cover your shame."

In the West, however, Christianity doesn't address the shame of Adam and Eve or the shame we bring upon our relationship with God. From an innocence-guilt perspective, Western Christianity teaches that the "garments of skin" God made signify the need for a blood sacrifice to pay for the guilt of sin, foreshadowing the sacrificial death of Jesus Christ. In connecting the story of Adam and Eve to the story of Jesus, Western Christianity neglects the glaring parallel that just as Adam and Eve were naked and ashamed as they ate the fruit that hung on the Tree of Knowledge of Good and Evil, Jesus was naked and ashamed as he hung on the tree of death.

In our twenty-first-century world—a world in which our communal existence has been reduced to a wasteland of broken relationships and distrust—we need a faith that not only addresses our guilt but also helps us deal with our shame.

I didn't have a close, personal relationship with my father as I was growing up. It's not that he was a negligent or absent parent; it's just that my father spent most of his time trying to regain the honor he'd lost as a child.

My father was born in the city of Lviv, Ukraine, in what may have been the most tragic year in Ukrainian history: "In 1933, Ukrainians died in the millions, in the greatest artificial famine in the history of the world."[38] Under the leadership of Joseph Stalin and his Five-Year Plan, the Soviet Union took possession of the Ukrainian countryside, forcing landowners to work as slaves and treating their crops as state property. By exporting millions of tons of grain from Ukraine, Stalin was able to accomplish two objectives: fund the industrialization of the Soviet Union and eradicate the peasant class of Ukrainians known as kulaks.

In his book *Bloodlands: Europe Between Hitler and Stalin*, Timothy Snyder writes,

Stalin had his "fortress" in Ukraine, but it was a stronghold that resembled a giant starvation camp, with watchtowers, sealed borders, pointless and painful labor, and endless and predictable death ...

A very few outsiders witnessed and were able to record what happened in these most terrible of months. The journalist Gareth Jones had paid his own way to Moscow, and, violating a ban on travel to Ukraine, took a train to Kharkiv on 7 March 1933. He disembarked at random at a small station and tramped through the countryside with a backpack full of food. He found "famine on a colossal scale." Everywhere he went he heard the same two phrases: "Everyone is swollen from starvation" and "We are waiting to die." He slept on dirt floors with starving children, and learned the truth. Once, after he had shared his food, a little girl exclaimed: "Now that I have eaten such wonderful things I can die happy."[39]

When the famine, the *holod*, as Ukrainians call it, came to an end, the horror was not over. In fact, for Central and Eastern Europeans, the horror was just beginning.

In the middle of Europe in the middle of the twentieth century, the Nazi and Soviet regimes murdered some fourteen million people. The place where all of the victims died, the bloodlands, extends from central Poland to western Russia, through Ukraine, Belarus, and the Baltic States ... The fourteen million were murdered over the course of only twelve years, between 1933 and 1945, while both Hitler and Stalin were in power. Though their homelands became battlefields midway

through this period, these people were all victims
of murderous policy rather than casualties of war
… Most were women, children, and the aged; none
were bearing weapons; many had been stripped of
their possessions, including their clothes.[40]

Hitler and Stalin brought unspeakable shame upon themselves,
their families, their countrymen, and the countless number of people
they violated.

As for those who suffered in the bloodlands, they endured with
the hope that the end of the Second World War would be the
beginning of freedom. However, in February 1945, when Franklin
Roosevelt, Winston Churchill, and Joseph Stalin—dubbed the Big
Three—met at the Yalta Conference to discuss war strategy and
postwar Europe, Roosevelt and Churchill agreed to give Stalin
control of Eastern Europe.

Once the war was over and the agreements made at Yalta were
put into effect, many Eastern European states that supported Allied
forces felt betrayed, and millions of Eastern European war refugees
refused to return home, afraid of the iron fist of the Soviet Union.

My father's father was one of those defiant refugees; he refused
to take his family back to Ukraine. During the war Soviet forces
had invaded Lviv and had taken possession of my family's house,
converting it into a hospital. Fearing death or deportation to a labor
camp, my family escaped from Ukraine, and my father's father
vowed they wouldn't return as long as their homeland was occupied
by the Soviet Union. Later, in 1950, when it became clear that
Ukraine would not gain its independence, the Hajduczok family
made its way to the United States.

The shame of it all—Stalin not being held accountable for
murdering millions of Ukrainians, the Big Three taking the liberty
of redrawing the map of Europe, and my family being stripped of
its wealth and honor—was too much for my father to accept, so for

the better part of fifty years my father committed his life in America to restoring what his family had lost in Ukraine.

Then, sometime around the year 2000, my father's world began to change as my mother's health deteriorated. What started with taxiing his wife from one doctor to another evolved into my father becoming a full-time caregiver. Twenty-four hours per day, seven days per week, my father monitored my mother's medications, prepared her meals, and escorted her every step. It got to the point that if my father was out of my mother's sight for more than a few minutes she would call out to him, panicked and pleading for him to come back.

As difficult as it all was, my parents survived, as did their marriage, and in 2008, they celebrated their fiftieth wedding anniversary. Our family and my parents' closest friends gathered to celebrate the occasion. The event included an informal ceremony, during which my parents renewed their wedding vows. After they both said, "I do," my father took a few minutes to talk about the ups and downs of life, to profess his love for his wife, and to publicly commit the rest of his days to caring for her.

In the two years that followed, my father tirelessly cared for my mother. He rarely had a full night's sleep, and when he got sick, he refused to see a doctor, not wanting to leave his wife. Then, in May 2010, on the verge of passing out, my father went to the hospital.

After a few days of testing, the doctors had a diagnosis: late-stage lymphoma. The condition was treatable, but a day or so later my father spiked a fever, and it was discovered he also had a systemic staph infection.

Realizing the seriousness of the situation, my three siblings and I went to see and be with our father. Hoping for the best but preparing for the worst, my father told each of us he loved us and said his goodbyes. Two days later, on the morning of June 2, 2010, Tato took his last breath and passed away.

Burdened by the shame of his past, my father spent most of his life chasing after honor. Yet in the end he finished well—he sacrificed his life for love.

When it comes to personal relationships, there is no greater way to express your commitment or to display your trustworthiness than to devote your life to the people you love.

In our twenty-first-century world—a world dying to control—I don't want to be "that guy" anymore, consumed by the shame of my past, trying to regain the honor that I lost in the garden of Eden, or in Ukraine, or who knows where some Friday night. I want to trust God, I want to believe my shame is covered, and I want to commit my life to loving others.

As for the essential, ever-present, unspoken question, "Do you trust me?"

I hope to be trustworthy.

I hope my daughters answer, "Yes."

ENDNOTES

1. Larry A. Samovar and Richard E. Porter, *Communication Between Cultures* (Stamford: Wadsworth, 2001), 27, 61.

2. "Developments in Aging 1967." A report of the Special Committee on Aging, United States Senate pursuant to S. Res. 20, February 17, 1967. Resolution authorizing a study on the problem of the aged and aging together with minority views, 113.

3. Ibid., vii.

4. Ibid., 112.

5. G. Van Groningen, *First Century Gnosticism: Its Origins and Motifs* (Netherlands: E. J. Brill, 1967), 15–16.

6. John Glyndwr Harris, *Gnosticism: Beliefs and Practices* (Portland: Sussex Academic Press, 1999), 108–11.

7. Alastair H. B. Logan, *Gnostic Truth and Christian Heresy: A Study in the History of Gnosticism* (Edinburgh: T&T Clark, 1996), 230–32; Charles W. Hedrick, *The Apocalypse of Adam: A Literary and Source Analysis* (Chico, CA: Scholars Press, 1980), 229—31.

8. Rev. Alexander Roberts and James Donaldson, ed., *The Ante-Nicene Fathers: Translation of the Writings of the Fathers Down to A.D. 325*, vol. 1, *Irenaeus Against Heresies*, book 2 chap. 23 by Irenaeus (Grand Rapids, MI: William B. Eerdmans Publishing, 1976), 551.

9. Rev. Alexander Roberts and Rev. W. H. Rambaut, trans., *The Writings of Irenaeus*, vol. 1 (Edinburgh: T&T Clark, 1974), 366.

10. J.N.D. Kelly, *Early Christian Doctrines*, rev. ed. (San Francisco: HarperCollins, 1978), 57.

11. Rev. Alexander Roberts and James Donaldson, ed., *The Ante-Nicene Fathers: Translation of the Writings of the Fathers Down to A.D. 325*, vol. 3, *Tertullian Against Marcion*, book 2 chap. 25 by Tertullian (Grand Rapids, MI: William B. Eerdmans Publishing, 1976), 316–17.

12. Rev. Alexander Roberts and James Donaldson, ed., *The Ante-Nicene Fathers: Translation of the Writings of the Fathers Down to A.D. 325*, vol. 3, *On the Resurrection of the Flesh*, chap. 61 by Tertullian (Grand Rapids, MI: William B. Eerdmans Publishing, 1976), 593.

13. Thomas P. Halton, ed., *Saint Augustine on Genesis: The Fathers of the Church: A New Translation*, vol. 84, *Two Books on Genesis Against the Manichees and On the Literal Interpretation of Genesis: an Unfinished Book, Against the Manichees*, book 2, chap. 22 by Augustine, Roland J. Teske, trans. (Washington, DC: The Catholic University of America Press, 1991), 129.

14. Ibid.

15. Martin Luther, *Luther's Commentary of Genesis*, vol. 1, chaps. 1–21, trans. J. Theodore Mueller (Grand Rapids, MI: Zondervan Publishing House, 1958), 86.

16. Ibid.

17. John Calvin, *A Commentary on Genesis*, trans. John King (London: The Banner of Truth Trust, 1965), 182.

18. Ibid., 183.

19. Gerhard Von Rad, *Genesis: A Commentary*, rev. ed. (Philadelphia: Westminster Press, 1972); U. Cassuto, *A Commentary on the Book of Genesis, Part I: From Adam to Noah*, trans. Israel Abrahams (Jerusalem: Magnes Press, 1961); John Skinner, *A Critical and Exegetical Commentary on Genesis* 2d ed., the International Critical Commentary (Edinburg: T &T Clark, 1930).

20. Von Rad, *Genesis*, 81, 97.

21. Cassuto, *Commentary*, 112–14.

22. R. Gordis. "The Knowledge of Good and Evil in the Old Testament and the Qumran Scrolls," *Journal of Biblical Literature* 76 (1957): 123–38; R. Gordis, "The Significance of the Paradise Myth," *American Journal of Semitic Languages and Literature* 52 (1935): 86–94; M. Noth and D. Winton Thomas, ed., *Wisdom in Israel and in the Ancient Near East*, vol. 3 of Supplements to *Vetus Testamentum*, 'Knowledge' of and 'Life' in the Creation Story, by I. Engnell (Leiden: E. J. Brill, 1955), 103–19; Bo Reicke, "The Knowledge Hidden in the Tree of Paradise," *Journal of Semitic Studies* 1 (July 1956): 193–201.

23. Reicke, "Knowledge," 196.

24. Noth and Thomas, *Wisdom*, 115.

25. Philip A. Schaff and Henry Wace, ed., *A Select Library of Nicene and Post-Nicene Fathers of the Christian Church*, second series, vol. 11, *Cassian's Conferences, The Third Conference of Abbot Chaeremon*, chap. 12 by John Cassian (Grand Rapids, MI: William B. Eerdmans Publishing, 1973), 428; Halton, *Saint Augustine on Genesis*, 129; A. Dillman, *Genesis: Critically and Exegetically Expounded*, vol. 1, trans. W.M.B. Stevenson (Edinburg: T&T Clark, 1897); Derek Kidner, *Genesis: An Introduction and Commentary* (Downers Grove, IL: Inter-Varsity Press, 1967); Franz Delitzsch, *A New Commentary on Genesis*, vol. 1, trans. Sophia Taylor (Minneapolis: Klock and Klock Christian Publishers, 1978); James Barr, *The Garden of Eden and the Hope of Immortality* (Minneapolis: Fortress Press, 1993).

26. Harold S. Stern, "The Knowledge of Good and Evil," *Vetus Testamentum* 8 (1958): 405–18; James Barr, *The Garden of Eden and the Hope of Immortality* (Minneapolis: Fortress Press, 1993).

27. Stern, "Knowledge of Good and Evil," 414.

28. Ibid., 415.

29. Halton, *Saint Augustine on Genesis*, 129.

30. Roberts and Rambaut, *The Writings of Irenaeus*, 366.

31. Von Rad, *Genesis*, 97.

32. Stern, "Knowledge of Good and Evil," 414.

33. Thomas Aquinas, *Summa Theologica of St. Thomas Aquinas*, vol. 4, Q. 183, Art. 2, trans. Fathers of the English Dominican Province (Allen, TX: Christian Classics, 1981), 1857–58.

34. Dietrich Bonhoeffer, *Dietrich Bonhoeffer Works*, vol. 3, *Creation and Fall: A Theological Exposition of Genesis 1–3*, trans. Martin Ruter and Ilse Todt (Minneapolis: Fortress Press, 1997), 142.

35. Ibid., 143.

36. Amy Harmon, "Prenatal Test Puts Down Syndrome in Hard Focus," *New York Times*, May 9, 2007; http://www.nytimes.com/2007/05/09/us/09down.html.

37. I first heard the term "maximizing discontinuity" from Brian McClaren at an emergent pastor's conference in San Diego in 2004. He used this term to describe how he closed his church for six months and reopened it under a new name with a new mission in order to definitively communicate that the new church was not an extension of the former church but a new entity with different goals and values, even though it would have the same pastor and some of the same people.

38. Timothy Snyder, *Bloodlands: Europe Between Hitler and Stalin* (New York: Basic Books, 2010), 19–20.

39. Ibid, 45, 47.

40. Ibid, vii–viii.